Poetry d'Amour 2015

Dear Nana & Pappa,

Merry Christmas!
Some of these poems might be not quite 'youthing' (a bit of swearing/graphic content) - but I think you might quite like the poem on Pg 22!
Love you as always and missing you loads.
Hug, kiss, & a whistle!
Love,
Megsy xxx ooo.

developing and promoting poets and poetry

Published November 2014 by

PO Box 684
Inglewood
Western Australia   6932

Email   wapoets@gmail.com

Website   www.wapoets.net.au

Facebook   www.facebook.com/poetry.damour

Copyright remains with the authors who assert all rights in relation to their work. Selection copyright 2014, WA Poets Inc.

Permission to reproduce any of these poems should be sought by initially writing to WA Poets Inc. at the above address. All enquiries will be forwarded to the relevant author.

Cover Art	*Of Love and Fate* by Beba Hall www.bebahallartist.com
Cover Design	Claire Bates Graphic Design www.clairebatesdesign.com
Layout	Gary De Piazzi

National Library of Australia Cataloguing-in-Publication entry

Title	Poetry d'Amour 2015 : love poems
ISBN	978-0-9873633-4-3 (paperback)
Subjects	Love poetry, Australian.
Other Authors/ Contributors	Chinna, Nandi, editor.
Dewey Number	A821.408

Poetry d'Amour 2015

love poems

edited by
Nandi Chinna

The poems in this anthology have been selected by Nandi Chinna from work by invited poets performing at Poetry d'Amour 2015, and from entries in the 2015 Poetry d'Amour Love Poetry Competition. Nandi Chinna judged the competition and kindly offered editorial suggestions.

Contents

Judge's Comments Nandi Chinna		7

2015 Poetry d'Amour Love Poetry Contest Award Winners
First Prize
    Jaya Penelope   **I Want To Send You**   9

Second Prize
    Anna Ryan-Punch   **Repeat**   10

Highly Commended
    Renee Pettitt-Schipp   **Autumn At The Cidery**   11
    Jaya Penelope   **The Bridge Of Birds**   12

Commended
    Gail Willems   **Anniversary**   13
    Rose van Son   **When She Was Well**   14

Greenhouse Realty Mandurah Award for the Peel Region
    Gail Willems   **Under The Orange Trees**   16

Remote and Regional WA Winner
    louisa   **Did I Disturb You?**   17

Youth Incentive Award
    Audrey El-Osta   **Persephone**   18

Poetry d'Amour 2015 Guest Poets
    Tom Lanoye   **Analysis**   100
    Concise Theory Of Evolution   102
    House-Training   104
    Poker   106
    Programme   108
    Rebellion   110
    Song Of Songs   112
    The Absence Of Hierarchies   114
    Mags Webster   **My First Kiss**   92
    Strange Vernacular   93
    Annamaria Weldon   **Untrue Distinctions**   94
    Sean M. Whelan   **They Don't Love Blue**   96
    This Is How It Works   98

Contents

Selected Poems: 2015 Poetry d'Amour Love Poetry Contest

Carolyn Abbs	The Boy From Grammar School	19
Atheer Al-Khalfa	Yes	20
Richard James Allen	Actually, Love	21
Meg Caddy	Tiddalik	22
Liana Joy Christensen	Evensong	23
	Soul Mate	24
Julie Clark	A Mother's Love	25
Rose Crocker	The Dream	26
Peter Curry	Crossing To Siberut	27
Cuttlewoman	Wildlife Documentary	28
Gary Colombo De Piazzi	Caught	29
	Intoxicated	30
Audrey El-Osta	If	31
	Pavlovian Conditioning	32
Frances Faith	Physical	33
	New Love Races	34
	Wait	36
	Writing You	37
Michelle Faye	Circular Reasoning	38
Kevin Gillam	What My Father Taught Me	39
Fran Graham	Beverages	40
	Black Forest Fervour	41
	Muse	42
	Tactical Sway	43
Danny Gunzburg	Where Are You Anne Holly?	44
Helen Hagemann	Conversation Hearts	45
	Travel Mementos	46
Lorraine Haig	If Love Was A Painting	47
Ron Heard	Historian	48
Ross Jackson	Marilyn With A Lute	50
	The Poet's Model	51
	Walking Marriage	52
Kerryn M. Kapitola	Las Estrellas De España	53
Christopher Konrad	Like Joseph And Aseneth	54
	Sex	56
	Speaking Portuguese	57
Deeksha Koul	River Eyes	58
Veronica Lake	Musical Buffet	59
Wes Lee	Eight Transitions	60
louisa	An Ordinary Man	61

Contents

Shey Marque	Desire Is Golden,	
	Like The Finch	62
Shane McCauley	Twenty Years Later	63
Fiona McIlroy	Last Day Of Floriade	64
	Love Boat	65
Max Merckenschlager	Humpback Hearts	65
Audrey Molloy	My Soul's Performance	67
	The Fossil	68
Annette Mullumby	Seaweed	69
	Teeth	70
	Trailing Clouds Of Glory	71
Karen Murphy	6 Months After My Friend	
	Hangs Himself	72
Jan Napier	Other People's Love Poems	73
K.K. O'Hara	Old Lace	74
Kirsty Oehlers	You Started As An Ember	75
Jaya Penelope	You Knocked Out My Walls	76
Rachael Petridis	Come Closer	77
Renee Pettitt-Schipp	Love Song	78
Margaret Owen Ruckert	In Love With An Ideal	79
Francesca Sasnaitis	Ghazal For An American	80
Tim Sladden	The Holding Pattern	81
Flora Smith	For My Brother	82
Elizabeth Tyson-Doneley	The Absence Of Holding	83
Tineke Van der Eecken	For Bert	84
	In Winter	85
Lyn Vellins	Dark Chocolates And Cherries	86
James Walton	Not Another Small Fucking	
	Love Poem	87
Julie Watts	This Is The Time I Like Best	88
Sunny Wignall	De Grey River	89
Gail Willems	Fingertips	90
Jena Woodhouse	Polydeuces	91

Biographies 116

2015 Poetry d'Amour Love Poetry Contest Judge's Comments

It has been my great pleasure to judge the 2015 Poetry d'Amour Love Poetry Contest. Many thanks to all those who submitted poetry to the contest, and with 236 entries it certainly was not an easy task to find the winning, commended and runner up poems. However, a winner must be chosen and there were a couple of standout entries. Love is a subject that is much written about and the challenge of the poet is to find new ways of saying old truths. The poems that stood out were able to show rather than tell, offered a fresh approach to an old story, and were able to maintain some burden of mystery; that is they did not attempt to answer all questions with trite or predictable endings, but offered an element of surprise and imaginative originality.

The winning poem is probably an unusual choice in that it is quite a short poem. But this poem really stood out for its stark beauty and powerfully appropriate use of metaphor. By using the metaphor of the trees 'holding blue eggs of ice in their hands', and the simple but strong ending 'how cold it's been' the writer invokes a desolation and sense of loss with so few words. This poem is like a clenched fist unfurling upon the page, to slap the reader with a blast of cold air and longing. The winning poem is 'I Want To Send You' by Jaya Penelope.

The overall runner up also stood out for its attention to form and strong metaphors; 'the chrysalis/we split by clasping hands'; and for its description of love that has endured, 'as if dropping years of coins into a money box'. It speaks concisely of love that is solid, affirmative and bountiful. I will hand it to you and say: feel this weight; look how we've grown', yet remains 'fresh as in butterflies, just like the first time'. The joy of the conclusion – at once concise and expansive, enables this poem to allude to the experience that cannot be captured by words and that the poet courts as a lover. The overall runner up is 'Repeat' by Anna Ryan-Punch.

The two highly commended: 'Autumn At The Cidery' by Renee Pettitt-Schipp is a beautifully described moment in time that the poet 'cannot own'. A quiet afternoon with a person they love, thinking about the idea of 'perfection' the poet describes being stunned and persuaded by the wind drifts of typha seeds. Again an original and totally personal reflection of an aspect of love. 'The Bridge Of Birds' by Jaya Penelope, speaks to the impossibility of the romantic ideal and the often momentary nature of the feeling of connection. The 'yawning hallway' separating love and the word, drifting across like a feather are evocative images that describe well the, 'impossible metaphor'.

Commended: 'When She Was Well' by Rose van Son, uses cooking and particular dishes as a way of describing the depth of a long term relationship and domesticity, with some lovely images such as 'the kitchen table barely strong enough to hold his arms around her', and, 'flowered tarragon to his lips her taste

2015 Poetry d'Amour Love Poetry Contest Judge's Comments

held on his tongue'. The rhythmic quality of the poem, enables the reader to entreat the senses and perceive the loving relationship.

'Anniversary' by Gail Willems, has a great sense of rhythm and form and uses original language such as ' In this light the canvas of skin has collapsed / the tent of your bones', and 'we fall into and out of each other / there is a separation between knowing and dreaming //. This piece expresses the mystery of love as something that cannot be pinned down, it is 'un-photographable'.

Greenhouse Realty Mandurah Award for the Peel Region: 'Under The Orange Tree' by Gail Willems. This poem takes the reader on a sensual journey, traversing time, in particular a Sunday that 'rises' and 'falls' evoking the sacred and transgression. As well as this the reader encounters landscape, 'at noon the choir of orange swung across the hillside' as well as the body and longing, 'the song of lust knew its way to stars'. The lyrical composition of this poem lends itself to the romantic and could easily have been lost to a saccharine ideal but the last line hooks a solid punch the lifts the reader to a delicious satisfaction.

Remote and Regional WA Winner: 'Did I Disturb You?' by louisa. This poem uses the architecture of the everyday to compose a scene of tenderness beyond the immediacy of love. The poem at first seems to be about the suffering of the loved one, 'The cord to your voice was broken', and become a homage to a different kind of love – that of the one who suffers in waiting to be able to love, 'I sat quietly on a stiff wooden chair'. A pleasure in love, forestalled, is also a type of offering and seduction.

Youth Incentive Award: 'Persephone' by Audrey El-Osta. This poem is perfectly situated in the transition between maidenhood and womanhood and uses the myth to be able to speak a truth of modern feminine experience; 'young lessons have been learnt, pleasure is no stranger'. Dividing the story between the seasons, not only respects the form of the original mythology but allows the reader to travel with the young 'demigoddess' as she brings 'back maiden grace to her garden'. The poem is playful, immediate and sensual – exactly as the winner of the youth section should be.

Nandi Chinna

Jaya Penelope　　　　　　　　　　*First Prize Winner*

I Want To Send You

this photograph of me
knee deep in snow by a frozen river.
See how the trees hold blue
eggs of ice in their aching hands?

How far I've come from that summer
of salt we woke wearing
each other's faces

how cold it's been?

Anna Ryan-Punch   *Second Prize Winner*

Repeat

It's everything I've already said;
repetition of words and looks
doesn't wear such gifts thin
but etches each more deeply:
like the constant love of water
carves liquid memory into rock.

Years have lived you along
to this day: parallel until our
perspectives met at the horizon.
You are so young to my eyes,
still damp from the chrysalis
we split by clasping hands.

Each of these words I will say again
as if dropping years of coins
into a money box. I will hand it
to you and say: feel this weight;
look how we've grown.
Our arms linked tight. Look, and how.

It's everything I've already said, and yet:
butterflies, just like the first time.

Renee Pettitt-Schipp   *Highly Commended*

Autumn At The Cidery

autumn
    we don't own it
        the way the sun is sleeping
                in the leaves
      sky boasting again about colour
    and our love like a clear note
just sung

we sit with all this
    and our tenderness curls like
        a satisfied cat
           gaze turned outward toward the river-gums
        where dragonflies move like laughter
    and butterflies descend
in slow sentences

and I am just about to think
    perhaps there is perfection
        only not sustained
           more like flashes
                of pure white light

        when seeds

soft stars
    begin
      falling
        falling
          constellations
              earth bound
                and shining

stunned in our seats
    lulled by pale ale
        pacified by their gentle persuasion;
            we let it happen
              a landscape taken by siege
                  the bulrushes
                      floating invasion.

Jaya Penelope *Highly Commended*

The Bridge Of Birds

The days when you stay
in your room and I in mine
the hallway yawns between us.

Weeks I tear my sheets to strips
weave swaying ladders of hair
send one word floating like a feather.

Whole months we do not look into
each other's eyes, not even as we lick
the salt from each other's skin.

Then, one night of the year the skies clear
and we reach for each other, one night
which could be any night the air is thick
with a flurry of feathers.

Wingtip to wingtip we span the spaces
between us, step lightly onto the back
of this impossible metaphor
meet for a moment on
the bridge of birds.

Gail Willems   *Commended*

Anniversary

In this light the canvas of skin has collapsed / the tent of your bones
a verandah door has unmade your height / I'll forget to notice
what language we use / the journey // you take a moment to breathe
half way up the track /a backdrop of ocean spindrift / Dampier's rose
listens to the waves / a beautiful noise measures distance.

Weaken me with your smile / hold out your hand
claim the space between my fingers / stroll hand in hand
marking a tempo / sensing winter's edge // your heart will circle
sever shadows at random / your kiss will hold the door open.

We fall into and out of each other / there is a separation
between knowing and dreaming // tonight I'll watch you sleep
trace pencil lead veins in your wrist / my fingerprints will imprint patterns
you / un-photographable.

Rose van Son   *Commended*

When She Was Well

When she was well, they made
ravioli, the table spread with little pillows

parcelled beef and herbs, spinach
cottage cheese, creamed pumpkin;

to fill the cone rolled off her tongue
a little nutmeg, just enough

to hold the light,
was all she wanted.

Her gift for him
chicken spiced with tarragon,

rolled and pinched, the spinach
squeezed   just long enough

to let green juices soak
the life that slips through squares

the kitchen table
barely strong enough

to hold his arms around her
as she leaned his way as best she could.

Remember me, she said, when she was well
her fingers greased to pinch those little pillows

her face to his and when the water boils
and bubbles rise as soon they must, breathe air

that gap between the water's pull
and lid, when strength takes all

those little pillows dropping in
take gasp, at first a shallow breath

but soon they swell   they float
her smile as he scoops them in;

Rose van Son *Commended*

her dimpled skin, aware of light
from light, burnt butter spread

flowered tarragon to his lips,
her taste held on his tongue.

Gail Willems *Greenhouse Realty Mandurah Award for the Peel Region*

Under The Orange Trees

the stones that I throw are picked up by the music of strings
in the sanctuary   Sunday rose from its bed of weeds
at noon the choir of orange swung across the hillside
scents sear in brilliant lines of fire   the naked form of you
under summer's long days tingles the air

the perfume of a weighty roundness
gets me all confused   leaves me damp
reaching for you

the song knew its way to stars
where night tethered itself to sky   the half-cast eye of a moon
lent dream filled nights the illusion of time

Sunday fades through a gate left ajar

I palm an orange   suck it dry

louisa *Remote and Regional WA Winner*

Did I Disturb You?

Did I disturb you,
Tiptoeing around your heart ?
It was dark
And seemed cold.
The cord to your voice was broken.
It looked like vandalism.
The guttering of your tears
Was rusty - full of holes.

I sat silently on a stiff wooden chair
Outside those metal doors.
I could smell the acrid fumes of welding.
Recent smoke.

I lit a fragrant candle.
I have my needle, thread and polishing rags,
I will wait.

Audrey El-Osta *Youth Incentive Award Winner*

Persephone

In summer Korei begins her time to bloom:
adolescent demigoddess grows quick with the moon,
learning slowly about men and women.
She sits alone and plays with her pearled oyster,
looking at *ikones* of Afroditi, touching her statues,
so beautiful, beautiful.
Her young lessons have been learnt, pleasure
is no stranger, not to young Korei.

In autumn Korei feels a change in her.
Innocent playtime now a ravenous hunger;
She patrols her domaine hunting as her *thea*
Artemis taught her, though not for wild stag.
She sees Hades above ground, and marks her prey,
strips her girdle free and leaves it in the garden:
For what she wants, she won't need it.

In winter, Korei knows her truth now.
Not a maiden anymore but a woman, a seductress
and underworld empress, a destroyer: let mortals
suffer my drought, I will get what I want.
Hades is my dark prince of chrome silver skin, cobalt eyes
stare into mine, loving every moment of my wild ride, hands
that tenderly guide the departed grip my hips with ravishing vigour.
Pleasure courses through the two gods,
earth shakes, nearly breaks to screams, whispers of
I love that, I love you.

In spring, Persephone rises, visits the earth
and brings back maiden grace to her garden
of youth. She finds nymphs and teaches them all
she learnt while she frolicked and fucked
in the underworld. Screams and giggles abound
as young maidens are women made
in the school of Persephone's touch.

Carolyn Abbs

The Boy From The Grammar School

Act one:
The day I turned fourteen   eye-level with the mirror
and boys   I locked the bathroom door,
tried a little hair lightener
on my fringe   gingerly at first   then
tipped it   all over my head   it fizzed and stung
fifteen minutes   for maximum effect.

My father called it   *Barmaid blonde!*
My mother said   *The nuns at school must never know.*
She took me to Annette's   perms, shampoos and sets.
Dye it brown, she said   and left.
I asked Annette   for **Black!**

Act two:
An underground coffee bar in town   banned
for convent girls, but
Maeve and me   checked the street   down shady stairs
        a cavernous space   dimly lit   crimson walls.
We ordered cokes   a corner table.
The boy from the Grammar School   collar turned up,
fed coins into the jukebox

                        the Crystals sang

            *Well he walked up to me
            and he asked if I wanted to dance...*

He glanced over   didn't recognize me at first
but when I whispered his name
he said, *I like your black hair*.
The song hung in the air:

            *And then he kissed me
            And then he kissed me...*

Atheer Al-Khalfa

Yes

Yes, let's now speak of love.
Speak of it as she walks back
Victorious,
Speak of her as it gets buried.
Yes, let's now speak with nothing,
Let's feel nothing,
Let's grieve with a perfectly flawless life;
Certainty has arrived, and with it futures' countless doubts.

Richard James Allen

Actually, Love

is the only thing that does last,
beyond the karmic astral space junk
drifting like detritus
from lifetime to lifetime
until it is finally worn into nothingness.

Love travels beyond lifetimes.
It doesn't just go on for eternity.

It is eternity.

Desire may be its currency,
and sex may be its pay dirt,
but love is the purpose of time.

Meg Caddy

Tiddalik

A Tadpole's Love Story

Love held me in a permeable membrane.
I was the eye of the river, rolling
past silver shrimp and weed-tongues.
When I wriggled free, wishing for lungs,
I found myself legless.

I moved like an ink-blot, swayed by waves
and the way sun looked like romance
splashed across the surface. A lustrous dance.
I found muddy secrets, and kissed river creatures –
hid myself from leeches.

Piece by piece, I devoured sonnet-flies
and ballad-beetles. I became bulbous,
bloated with briny lies. My feet
burst from my body and pushed me towards light.

When I had frog-legs and wide hands,
I gaped and swallowed words –
a creek of love-songs and laments
warmed my belly, wrapped me
until my head was love-stuffed,
and I finally had enough.

Love bubbles from my lips.

Liana Joy Christensen

Evensong

The earth shows traces
you have passed this way;
like the bandicoots
feasting on ant honey,
I shall sip from
the smile of your furred belly
watching the smile
rise in your eyes
until your lids tremble
like leaves on the bushes
where the numbat has vanished
unseen.

        Fire, spike of balga
        catching gold tossed
        from raceme to raceme
        among the Christmas trees
            — outshining the day.
        Come to me like limestone
        sweet water
        fretwork labyrinths
        lift me up to the southern cross
        and lay me down on the cool sands
        of eventide where the susurrus of the
        southern ocean shall be
        our night prayer.

Liana Joy Christensen

Soul Mate

Who but you on your board this morning
all salty and smiling and waving *hi*

Who but you on the school verandah standing out
from your mates in non-standard jumper

Who but you dares front the teacher *the Dire Wolf
got a bad rap — looks innocent to me*

Who but you with your schoolboy heart and man's
hands on the beach this evening

Who but you in me?

Julie Clark

A Mother's Love

Love is fighting with your siblings to sit on your mother's lap
Getting a kiss on the cheek as she tucks you in for a nap
The smell of her lipstick and the slight hint of Tweed perfume
The feeling of prettiness wearing a dress she has sewn
Having a cooked breakfast every day and a warm ironed shirt
Knowing she loves you even when you are covered in dirt
As the years go by becoming best friends and reminiscing
Sharing her wisdom, stories, a brandy and just listening
Then as she gets older her mind still alert her body is frail and weak
You become her and tuck her in at night and kiss her on the cheek
Comforting, cooking and caring for her till one night she slips away
Knowing her love will stay with you forever you'll miss her every day

Rose Crocker

The Dream

> *based on the novel 'The Dream' by Emile Zola, about the doomed love between a wealthy aristocrat's son and an embroider obsessed with sainthood. She eventually starves herself to death in the belief that this will bring her closer to God.*

Await my tenderness, angelic one.
Clouds bloom, if you watch them,
if you prick yourself
in these endless seas of grass.
Then, so spacious. My heart filled every corner,
bright fungus of the hour, expanding
life through the cracks.

Now, the high light shifts and flickers
from window to wall.
And I am curled, first in the dark cathedral's shell,
second, in the blankets we harvested as cloud.
Watching, the world's only belonging,
the sun's projection moans.
My flesh falls from the bone.

Peter Curry

Crossing to Siberut

Now I remember –

Yes.
At the rise of the moon
We departed from the harbour;
Little more than kids we were, on our kick-ride back to the Stone Age in sneakers –

By old diesel pulse your sighs returned to me
And I forgot those skies lit up by a gibbous moon,
And I thought of nothing but your sweet side, your ragged breath held upon my breath –

Like breath to be held for such a short time, you said –

Later, I sat up at the prow
To go forgetting you in the sea air once again
To watch gossamer fish fly forward, in the crazy glint of that moon –

We told stories, of such love as we had known
And I reported our joy and our sorrow doled out in equal measure,
Recalling you again as the diesel grunted, turning and turning the screw –

We slept. In the morning we braved bark boats,
Hitting land much quieter than we had been at sea.
The forgetful ocean, the lilt of the ship on the wine-dark waves drawing speech –

Thus it was. I thought I had forgotten all of this.
Yet I now conjure memory from the loss of our old regard,
Even when our love has long since forgotten, turning itself into stone –

Gone is our friendship, gone is the swell,
Gone is the sea-moon that watched over our crossing,
Gone knowing that a ship can never cross the same dark ocean twice –

But ending? No. I know of no such thing;
Only passing, and change, and what new life brings into being.
That will too pass without stones or poems to mark that it ever was.

Cuttlewoman

Wildlife Documentary

I. Monday

I remove sticks from my hair.
I know I have lived today.

II. Tuesday

As I step from the shower
A caterpillar falls out of my pubic hair.
I know I have lived today.

III. A month later

That racket?

It is just a gentleman with schizophrenia
snoring in the shed, snoring so loud
I am shaken out of bed.

I know I will live today.
I feel it in wan laughter
seeping from the liver.

IV. A year later

My love said, *I need you, I want you,*
This is the way it was meant to be.
So we entered into polygamy
With one night for her and a night for me.

And then I found I could not do it
(Nor it.) I had not the throw for it,
not the culture, not the underpinnings
of reciprocal relationships,
not the compassion for the other woman.

I am stranded in an impossible bend of the river.
Still singing whilst drowning,
still eating rotting rivery things.

I guess I must have lived today.
There is a flopping flapping thing here with me.
A sign: The head is not yet dead.

Gary Colombo De Piazzi

Caught

The kitchen smells
simmer slow movements;
carry ingredients and aromas
mingling under everyday touch;
build and cascade, tempt
the taste of memories savoured.

You move close,
        I can almost taste you.
The maturity of age with its depth
of flavour draws out the sharp tang.

You move with a comfortable ease
and my eyes follow your swagger
                around the kitchen.
There is a lilt to your step
and a song in your eye
as you catch me watching.

        Easily slip a smile
and manoeuvre
as steam rises from your pot
        a brew for two.

Old affections;
the depth of your voice;
the embrace
        in your eyes
the contours
                of your lips.

I was hooked before I knew
the word freedom
and now after years
of straining against your line
                you reel me in.

Gary Colombo De Piazzi

Intoxicated

I awaken to adore each breast
slip beyond the crease of doubt
        and fall into the endlessness
                of your kiss.

        Falter at the roundness
of hips and delve into
                the tease of your hair.

In the intoxication of you
I lose all sense of hours and days;
adrift on the memory of lips.

        Lost in the intensity of you
each inconsequential breath
rises in steps to grasp
                what life remains.

That instant stretched to an eternity
        and you in the sweat and tangle
        with a slight smile and elsewhere eyes;

        until there is nothing but lips.

Audrey El-Osta

If

If
for some reason
you were to end it all
with me
tomorrow morning;
I go to bed tonight
nestled in your arms
knowing I am so happy
to have known you
and would not trade
any of it for peace
of mind or mended
heart.

If
for some reason
I had to end it all
with you
tomorrow morning;
fall asleep my darling,
know that I have loved you
with purest and deepest heart
and clear intentions
and I know you love me
as we rub noses and share breath
for this our last night.

If
For some reason
The universe found cause
to separate us;
stay strong and know that
our time together
was a gift and should we find one
another again, then
it is truly meant to be.

If
for some reason
everything goes according to plan;
and we lay in each other's arms day after day
remain in the truest love and stay together;
know that I have pondered every alternate universe,
and in even the darkest timeline
I have always returned to you
and you have always found me.

Audrey El-Osta

Pavlovian Conditioning

Do you know the story of Pavlov and his dog?
He fed the hound meat daily, and noticed salivation
before he lay the plate down. He began to ring a bell
before he lay the plate down and soon enough a bell
made the dog salivate without any food in sight.

She learnt about classical conditioning in high school
psychology; a student of mind and behaviour long
               before university.
She liked a boy, chose him as her mark and baked
for him every day, fresh cookies. Two hundred grams
of salted butter, half that brown sugar, two eggs, two
cups flour, a teaspoon of baking powder, and a whole
packet chocolate chips, sweet kisses for joy and love.

Everyday for one spring week, a dozen cookies baked, two
went to her sisters, two to her mother, one for each best friend.
Leaving four warm, crumbly, crunchy,
               soft on the inside, biscuits for her dream boy.

Everyday for one spring week, they would talk and flirt,
she would feed him and he would eat until she could be sure,
absolutely sure that he associated her, face and body with the
feelings of joy that came when you ate chocolate chip cookies.
Freshly baked,
               just for you.

She asked him over one week later, and he came to her house
where she made pancakes covered in Nutella, he ate breakfast for
               the first time in years.
    I liked you long before you made the cookies, you know.
Why didn't you ask me out, why did you wait?
    Suddenly, there were cookies. I like your cookies.

Frances Faith

Physical

We are
carbon-based life-forms
eking out existence on a
rock fragment soon to be
obliterated by the sun...
relatively speaking.

How odd,
how unscientific,
that we should amass
quantities of affection
for one another,
randomly,
in the finite neurons
and chemical concoctions
of our anatomy.

How shall we rationalise
such bizarre behaviour
to our progeny, and theirs,
who will surely demand
an explanation?
Particle. Lepton. Boson. Quark.
Love by any other name
doth bind as sweetly.

Frances Faith

New Love Races

New love races
as the smile and wink
chase, giggle and blush in a
frantic domino trail to that
first touch.

It notices loose threads
lipstick colour
shiny shoes
hair curls.

Teeth gleam minted in anticipation.
New love perches on eager toes
eyebrow raised
waiting in tuxedo for
madam to order.

Diamond eyes
prize any word
uttered and raised
to mystery worth the most
earnest pondering.

New love is pumps.
Old love is slippers.

Old love shuffles
stops before the curio window
to gaze vacantly at oddments.
Seen them before.
Somewhere?

It forgets conversation
birthdays
whatever it was
that made you laugh.

Yesterday's tee shirt is good enough.
Old love rolls over
turns the page
changes the channel
lets the cat out in a blizzard.

Frances Faith

Tired eyes
take in the same old
view. Hardly worth asking,
What was it you said?

Frances Faith

Wait

You are standing by the rail,
looking as you always do
to the horizon slicing
the earth in two.
My heart watches your vigil
while it carries the daily
burden of my blood.
Your gaze anchors us both.
Where would you go
were it not for the rail
holding you?
Your love is a promise
spoken to the distant line,
mine a cloak around us
as we wait to meet it.

Frances Faith

Writing You

Write him! they insist.
Describe his chest, his lips, his eyes!
They see my love-drunk smile and tease.
Cupid's Fool! Give us verse to prove your passions;
and I wilt,
suddenly too aware of
the creases in my knuckles
and the grain of the paper.

They bay for the blood of my pen,
thirsty as Pharaoh's tomb
for words of immortality.
I measure word after word
and find every one
too puny
too trite
too flimsy a resource to write
you.

My fingers stroke the page,
journaling with trembling the chapters,
the volumes they hold,
remembering your skin,
your hair;
trying to translate ink-less to
empty lines
the contours of your body,
the shape of my delight.
The sheet before me
shimmers with countless shapes
defying language.

I write a sonnet
to satisfy their hunger;
phrases embalmed with myrrh and cinnamon
to decorate their ideas.
I am released then
wearing Sphinx smile,
content to write you
wordlessly.

Michelle Faye

Circular Reasoning

1. Today she is wading
                  treading water,
   through pieces of blue
   coloured ceramic that a moment ago
   formed her favourite vase!
   Now a maze for bare feet,
   she reaches for the keys and in one breath
   the other screams
   I-HATE-YOU-DON'T-LEAVE-ME.

2. Tonight she feels the weight of a body
   in the dark, eyes do not see   lips, lines, teeth
   all lost to blurry shadow
   but for the faint (and feint) of heart
   the outline of shoulders
   moving above, fingers at hips, the soft brush
   of eyelashes on cheeks.
   It is in the thick air they share their
           inhales and   exhales
   in time
   she accepts sex as silent apology.

3. Today they stand side-by-side,
   squeeze one another's hands,
   all smiles as the salesman returns,
   a swatch of colours for them to umm
      err and ahh over.
   They choose Sinatra Blue and keep moving
   through the paces, down the path
   set out for them, to make life easy
   to follow the arrows
   but ignore all the signs,
   laugh and kiss at the final checkout,
   so easily convinced somehow.

Kevin Gillam

What My Father Taught Me

was to eat an apple to its core and
find
infinity in the home and walk,
walk it
out and abbreviate, to say *well, April's*

nearly over on the 20th
of the month and sing Gregorian
chant
in falsetto while vacuuming,

to rub the bark of a tuart, to sweep,
pack away, put away, waste not, want not,
not drink,
but, in later years, to enjoy

a glass of Merlot, make music
in the absence
of light and score,
confuse watering the roses
and being, sip
from sky and silence

Fran Graham

Beverages

When we wake in the morning I drink
coffee and my lover drinks tea. At night
we enjoy wine. She prefers red, I think
I'm less prone to headaches if I drink white.

Our relationship is quite new. I come
from a year of grieving over my last
one; she, from twelve solo years, and quite numb
from the preceding violent ones. How fast

we fell in love, and the wonder of it,
stuns us still. A miracle, we both say,
at sixty-one, and her, straight. We have lit
up each other's life. We intend to stay

that way, sharing tea and coffee before nine
and at night, make love over a glass of wine.

Fran Graham

Black Forest Fervour

The hour and a half that separates us
holds the thought balloons
of our silent conversations.
They float across suburbs,
snippets plucked by the exultant
and those hungry for love.
The air distils the echo of our sighs,
rippling the ether like frost crackling,
the sound, light as a leaf,
our longing, solid as a paperweight.

The night descends in layers;
a fascinator of netted mist,
whipped cream and kirsched cherries.
Time dawdles,
puts together the raw ingredients,
builds our torte of faith and fantasy,
slabs spiced with honeyed impatience.

On the top we are dancing
amidst streetlight frosting
and shards of midnight chocolate.
Above us,
a confetti of stars.

Fran Graham

Muse

There you are my future muse
nothing like I thought you'd be.
Surprised, I gather different clues
consoled to find you're so like me.

Craving builds a head of steam
the fragrance of your wild red hair
I quietly wrap and tag the dream
and long to see you everywhere.

We hang together spirit-fixed
smile agreement, chat away
our steady start, a fabric mixed
with fragile light, still drying clay.

My hopes are colour-focused now
and agile, like a mermaid's tail.
Belief becomes my solemn vow
elaborate myth and holy grail.

This new terrain is mystery sweet
a lavish spread, endurance tough
strong and firm beneath my feet
a developing theme but still, enough.

Fran Graham

Tactical Sway

The outside lamp is the moon
in humid summer's dark humming
as we rock in a spot-fire embrace.

Seeds furrow in early whisperings
yield rhythms of warm breath
perfect like leaves in cool shadow.

I am ambitious but say nothing;
she construes my silence as empty
but it is bursting with significant muteness.

Secretly I'm a woman on the move
but a practised patience slows me,
my breasts against hers heavy with longing.

My head is a mosaic of lizard quick thoughts
unconcerned about their happy movements
and glossed quick-sliver flashes.

Desire carves itself
Into my distraction; carving deeper
than genius and lost thought.

I step out into half a mile of possibilities
measure them against my dreams growing
as lavish as a footprint in snow.

I am tempted to stop breathing just to feel
and nothing more but instead I swallow
the whole conspicuous evening.

Danny Gunzburg

Where Are You Anne Holly?

In the morning I called you,
not with the phone,
but with my mouth into
the azure sky.
My heart danced around a leaf
and sent a smoke signal to
your Bayswater house.
Where are you Anne Holly?
What are your eyes doing today?
Your small hands and your pink mouth,
what bell does your soul ring?
The hymn of your smile and your round
hips.

I am lost to this music,
I am lost to this doubt;
to the dance, the hope,
the broken telephone of "no".

Anne Holly give me one more chance
to sing you to the mountain,
and lay upon the chair of youth.

Let six islands be your hair,
let five moon beams be your mouth,
have eleven elephants bring your heart beat
to me on a crazy trampoline.

It's only a song, and I will write it on your
hands like the moon was a minister
of God.

Helen Hagemann

Conversation Hearts

Saturday night on the rocky
        shores of the east coast.
Love is confectionery, sweet musings
     taking place on the bus,
        in the shake of a bag.
Not even the atmosphere of ten miles
     to a movie disturbs the party
        in your mouth.
You crack hug me into chalky bits,
     suck lucky lips over cloud nine,
        chew cutie pie into spikes.
Each heart seems a milestone in your life,
     honey breaks from moon,
        wedding from cake.
All you can do is roll the tongue over
     its sweet nature, remembering
        a fractured night far off.
Someone singing in the branches, dream
     boy on the grass, the sugary kiss
        of real love on the mouth.

Helen Hagemann

Travel Mementos

for Lucas North (1973-2013)

Wherever we went,
I brought one home,
a mug, teaspoon or book filled
with the memories of our travels.

Of all the fridge magnets
on the door, you said.
There's too many. What do you
want them for?

To recount where we've been, I said
what we did and saw.
I pointed to the Del Rio pelican
in the Hawkesbury scene.

Remember the kangaroos crowding
the golf course at dusk?
From the top of a kitchen shelf
I lifted a candle, dark as a pint of ale.

And look! These four magnets
mapped our circling through the mountains,
from Ocean Beach to Patonga,
from Saratoga to Umina.

And here's the riverboat at Spencer,
our last stop before a treacherous climb,
those boggy edges slipping us
to my brother's Hunter Valley farm.

Left on your desk now, a curled notebook;
sodden rain caught us camping in November.

The bright glow of your frame survives, the
day you slipped an arm around the bronzed
Solomon Wiseman. Your cap angled on his rigid
head, bringing the green back into your eyes.

Lorraine Haig

If Love Was A Painting

If love was a Van Gogh
I'd want to touch its skin
to feel the ridges of the paint
and drink the colours in.

If I wanted to love danger
it's a Caravaggio.
How I'd love to be adrift
in the darkness of its shadow.

If love was a Vermeer
it would be my addiction
in a room of light and nuance
left guessing its intention.

If my days seemed a confusion
my dreams an empty echo,
if I had a melancholy perspective
I'd be in love with a de Chirico.

If love was a Matisse
I'd be out en plein-air
lying naked in the sun
yellow daisies in my hair.

If I loved a wild imagination
painted terrors in the void,
tormented figures in a landscape
it would be an Arthur Boyd.

Ron Heard

Historian

We hadn't yet said
words of commitment
but went to lunch
at Jimmy Watson's
usually too expensive for students.

Loud lawyers at the bar;
we find a corner of the courtyard
next to two academics
in quiet conversation.

We share bouillabaisse   aioli
crusty bread
and glasses of French Chablis.

We talk of everything

pour more wine;

we are silent
overhear
*Marsden   Macarthur
Macquarie*
and you whisper
that's Manning Clark.

I am not sure
all grey-bearded historians
look alike;

the bouillabaisse is rich and sweet

the wine is stony dry,
your eyes are an impossible intermixture
of green and brown.

When he leaves
the man who might be Manning Clark
offers us the rest
of his wine

Ron Heard

says
*I couldn't help noticing
the way
you've been
intertwining fingers.*

Ross Jackson

Marilyn With A Lute

> *I am trying to find myself. Sometimes that's not easy.*
> Marilyn Monroe

An exclusive collection of original photographs from LA
on the way to the display, memories of my first nude,
the Swedish girl from Summer with Monika,*
who like the dark haired teenager Norma Jean
was not yet in debt to kohl or scarred by crimson.

With thicker waists, hips and thighs, much more to hold
than the sinewy coat hangers of today.
For so long these two honey-haired girls
have remained in a place of mine
which has not yet been visited by therapists.

The photographic survey of Miss Baker,
Mrs Dougherty and the other forsaken
more severely blonde married ladies
begins with Marilyn as teen model in pointiest of bras
but ends with a product oversold by Warhol.

Somewhere in between, an odd one out
Titled-*Marilyn with a Lute*.

When sitting for that picture, awkward musician
she looked just as lost
as I have been for fifty years and should I reach ninety-five
I expect that somewhere in the rear
she and Monika will still be shuffling about.

*Summer with Monica was a 1953 film directed by Ingmar Bergman shown at The Village Continental Cinema, Dalkeith as part of the International Film Theatre series (1968).

Ross Jackson

The Poet's Model

As I'd plate her tiny lunch
she'd sit for me
in the lounge chair
its castors sunk into carpet
window light washing her eyes
brightening linen flowers.

I held back details of my little life
whilst cuttings of news from her garden
is what she'd offer up
and spill every second week at least
crumbs the cleaner received from someone else.

I'd do her bit of shopping
then in the overheated room
make a study of her nodding off.
A mirror, easy reference once she'd gone
for such details as fine hair, pale eyes.

Well Mum, after so many sittings
finally: this poem.

Ross Jackson

Walking Marriage

Headed home by Runners World
careering north   doing our walk
along the number nineteen bus route
grooving our marriage gaits
on our daily afternoon reunion.

Across the road at the tennis complex
corellas snowy camellias
in the pines.

We haul past the doctor's
step over a pizza box upturned
cheese and scarlet
slime the pavement surface.

Pepsi rocks, Taj Mahal
a poster covered hotel wall
shrieks at us.

In step we approach the corner
the jumbo chip bucket atop
the chicken shop
rotates aloft its same old
franchise stripes.

At the end of our commute
there will be clothes to iron, wood to chop
everything but *Work*.

And intimated, yet unspoken
Cup of tea?
is the sweet, routine thought
settling us down Walcott Street.

Kerryn M. Kapitola

Las Estrellas De España
The Stars Of Spain

I loved you in a language that I didn't speak,
And watched your lips form words and kisses,
And your eyes burned behind the colour of melting chocolate,
They spoke in a tongue that I couldn't misinterpret.

I held you on the beach under the Spanish sky
       (the sand in our shoes,
       our drinks in the sand)
I muttered phrases in simple vocabulary
You smiled and knew what I meant.
I shivered, I laughed, I clung,
And you asked me,   *"Por qué?"*
My mouth twisted with uncommon intonation and whispered into your warm neck,
– that cocoa stubble on cinnamon skin –
        "Estoy feliz."
They were words that held too much meaning,
       heavy like a sponge, saturated and leaking.
I had not the expression in English, nor Spanish, to say any more.
           You pulled me closer and held my waist and touched my face,
            and found my mouth with your own - articulation be done with.

Only the stars of Spain bore witness,
And by the Spanish sea, was forged a secret.
And to their questions, I lied.

Because you were my language, the one I could never speak.

Christopher Konrad

Like Joseph And Aseneth

*Your name shall no longer be called Aseneth, but your
name shall be called City of Refuge**

I
He had forgiven her: her and her priests
sand had become his time, the road his library, his Shibboleth.
He wondered about her table manners, her books, her shoes
about their house together, feathers and gravel.
Her eyes opened wide to him, took him in: orphan boy
gave him shelter, a reason to die, a wage for his sanity.
Until one day she had a dream of honeycomb on her lips
when her flesh became like flowers from a walled-in mother-city
until her bones were strong like cedar, her sex a black mourning dress.

He sought her forgiveness because he was unworthy, walked barefoot
into people's homes, blessed or cursed them: he became a eunuch
for her and began sailing merchant ships, gun running, an army deserter
writing poems that would change the world: bees settled on her mouth
blessings bestowed on many men and women
she became a walled mother-city
and her name became City of Refuge
in pregnant beauty arrayed with too many questions for one lifetime.

II
The rains washed down Manna from dark skies
water trickled in our rusty, leaf-filled gutters
insects burrowed up from out of the ground
and bird call from all over: a cacophony on the morning.
You had stood motionless in the heat of the preceding days
honeycomb on your lips
bees pointing the way back to your mouth:
I remembered the unfilled parking lot where we sat all that day
long ago   sat talking, being, loving
and thereafter whimsical empty summer Sundays, movies, cafes.
It was an apocalypse of honey, our meeting
as if you were the daughter of a priest
and I the local carpenter.

Christopher Konrad

The cross of our alphabet, stars shouted our ancient names;
foreigners that we were to each other
other-language speakers, even after the flood,
the downpour of uneven bread
the honeycomb strong on your lips
the bees a halo, a Medusa and I shaking
in the field after being stung all over
waiting for succour from your sweet kisses.

* From the apocryphal Jewish tale *Joseph and Aseneth*

Christopher Konrad

Sex

Is there anyone out there for me?
The singer sings her song
Which is a song for sex
The body wants what the body wants
She sings   what the body needs, perhaps.
But I remember my younger days these days
Paths   journeys   travels.
Whatever   sex is sex;
Some get it   got it   some don't or wont;
The whole package   flotsam upon a sea of sensual jetsam.
Kundera calls it *l'amour*
I don't know about that
Sometimes I think it's just about *want someone;*
Want something   the itch that can't be completely scratched.
Do I need love?   maybe: I won't whitewash it though
The body wants what it wants
Then I can leave maybe not.
Get caught in the synaesthesia of it all;
By your look, by your *savoir fare* of eye, voice, hair
I don't know   maybe by your choice of shoes
Maybe I just want to know I can love;
Or to love and to leave to love again and again
Maybe one person can't ever be the one for me,
I heard him say one sunny afternoon
The body wants what the body wants.

Christopher Konrad

Speaking Portuguese

> *Like a friar, I'm going to undie of stone.*
> Manoel de Barros

If I could speak like Manoel de Barros
I would write a Portuguese love poem
Because there, in Brazil, on the edge of the Old World
Cusp of the New, you can love many women.

I would write countless lines like:

    #1: she looks upon me from a constellation
           makes a gift of her skin

    # 2: she is round on my mouth
           is a sun splinter in my eye
           slides off my words like a cascade

    #3: he is ochre of play here to linger
           trace of honey and auburn through my fingers

I sift through many dictionaries   other languages
find some definitions like:

        Weight of breath   colour of voice
        Scent of deflated demeanour
        Salt of soft word on molasses evenings

In Portuguese all these things are possible
where love can fill any house
even when you're not there
because, somehow, you are everywhere
in the sound, sight, smell of each room.

Deeksha Koul

River Eyes

The rain again in late autumn.
I am to meet you in a café. It is mid-afternoon.
I enter. You are seated near the corner, wearing a woollen sweater.
Wafting of brewing coffee. Inside warmth.
The lights are dimmed. Your legs are crossed.
You cannot see me but you will know my heat.
You are arched over, reading, poetry perhaps.
You will want to discuss it with me. You look up.

Veronica Lake

Musical Buffet

If music be the food of love, let's feast!
I'm looking for a surfeit, an excess
upon which to glut myself with feeding.
Bring me no songs of sad melancholy;
I'll have no dying fall, no tearful tune.
Let harp strings echo trembling heart
and disco rhythms pulse into the night.
Let air resound with lordly symphonies,
chorals and the blast of heavy metal.
Let trills cascade, like waterfalls,
overflowing with passion.
Sound the trumpets! Let there be fanfares,
and good vibrations, thrumming up my spine
Let beating drums swell to a crescendo
where Valkyries sing in exultation
and all the music of the spheres rings out
in celebration of love's sweet madness.
For music does my love augment with fire,
provides a score seductive with desire.

Wes Lee

Eight Transitions

A teacher somewhere holds on to a drawing of yours –
a sperm grown to a foetus in eight transitions.

It was the flavour then for metamorphosis.
She put her hands over your eyes.

You were clowning at the blackboard
and did not know she had entered the room. Miss Pivac

with her skinny knees, her Russian cigarettes,
had sat on the desk and recited Auden.

The desk whose grooves have now become
the lines you would like to follow back

along the fork (of this very long lifeline)
and listen again to the love she spoke directly to you.

louisa

An Ordinary Man

She had always wanted
a knight in shining armour.
And he came.
He was balding
and wore glasses.
His moustache lived above his gentle voice.
He held the hand of the glass woman.
He listened as she shattered
into a thousand pieces.
He quietly swept them up and patted her back into shape.
He bought jewels you cannot touch.
He left pearls in her heart.
He took nothing but his leave.
He gave her the sword to slay her dragons.
He was
just
an ordinary
man.

Shey Marque

Desire Is Golden, Like The Finch

I don't mind the quiet in a nest
can learn to like solitude   think of it as the distance between notes
                             and in reverse   the same can be said
insert melody into silence singing in this cage of ribs
only   your long absences are harder to fill
          with excuses   or the song of finches.

To the silence of infinity   we walk at right angles
toward a landscape so set in reverse
even music cannot find its way
to carve such absence on trees   in which finches hang
          upside down and mute from branches
          ring barked by desire for larger fruit.

Curves are all that is left over   the reverse of a letter I
carved your absence into yesterday's ghost gum
sensuality of torso   stroked by finch feather
silence grafted onto my own body
like the bean that swells inside
sweet twin   Stradivarius.

In reverse sense   you and I are near
          vena umbilicalis carry my blood to him
we share pitch and rhythm
listen to the Doppler (absence of silence)
my little dog yaps to the galloping hoofs
while finch wings flutter on rousing.

This frenzy of presence   rests in silence
unspoken   because my message
if delivered by words   becomes reversed
creates but a string   of spongy symbols
absence soaking up a certain view
asking to be taken the wrong way.

On the floor
beside my Moroccan writing desk
a finch's nest   filled with paper eggs
cracks in their shells
the scratching and writhing inside   silence is dying
spheres of doubt   hatching absence.

Tiny finch beaks open and close in silence
          absence has its meaning reversed
          because all embryonic form contains momentum.

Shane McCauley

Twenty Years Later

We thread ourselves through time
let the days bloom around us
while they can and notice
at midday that our shadows
on the grass have become one.
Without going anywhere we have come far
seen many things with shared eyes
tasted all that we can together
dreamt the other while apart.
There is no more to ask than that.
The only darkness is clasped warm
in our hands as we step unhurriedly
through the seasons while always
counting down to Spring. We look
back along the hard dry ridges and
leafy paths and fault-lines all
the surprises of our voyaging
that have brought us to here
that have brought us to now
that have brought us so quietly
and constantly to the other
almost perhaps a work of art
with a few small flaws and frayed edges
but having avoided the ways
time can bankrupt the heart
wear down the brightest love
on grinding stone or reshape it
as if on potter's wheel or
whisper sinisterly in caves of night:
borrowed time borrowed time borrowed time.
We are each other's time
and we are in it as the new green seeds
share the sheltering and nurturing pod.
Twenty years and we still travel
within the other's endless universe
untiring and staunch and unrelenting
not taking time for time we know takes us
but smiling the other's smile and
being at last at last content.

Fiona McIlroy

Last Day of Floriade

all those nodding heads;
poppies, violas, tulips,
will tonight, so we heard,
be mown down in their prime
by the grim reaper, symbol
of our time, since after all;

we in the capital must not see
the fullblown rose, her petals fall
her unkempt hem, at all cost
we must preserve the illusion
of permanence, of status quo.

Such a colourful spring we had
you and I
a spring that made my blood sing
but no summer came
our harvest was not to be.

Today we politely nod heads
over rye bread,
note that the kites
were a bit
of an anti-climax,
faces strained with trying
to smile, to relax;

drained of colour now
all flowering cut down

our floriade is over.

Fiona McIlroy

Love Boat

Was it the crescent moon
lying on her back
inviting slow seduction;

was it the elephant
cleverly constructed
from ship towels
asking for destruction;

was it the descent into
sleep lulled by Mozart's
concerto twenty-one

that led our lips to tango?
Or was it the Pacific
gently rocking our queen

bed till all resistance
dissolved, as coral
atolls lit up the cave?

Was it the breaking free of
glaciers further south that
convinced us to be brave?

Was it the unspoken need to be
lifted on a wave of sensation
that rocked our residual fear;

or the moonlight sonata
of renewed desire; the allure
of the French tongue in Noumea

that woke us in the night
alive to one another?

Max Merckenschlager

Humpback Hearts

> *On Aug 22nd 2008 an injured 4.5m Humpback whale --*
> *affectionately named Colette -- was put down by veterinarians*
> *after being discovered in shallow waters north of Sydney. The*
> *calf was found motherless and starving in Pittwater, nuzzling*
> *yachts as she searched for her mother.*

You broke our hearts, Colette, we anguish yet.
When circumstance seduced your liege,
maternity was transferred to a passing hull.
Instinctively the phantom fish was tracked.

We can't forget your liquid sighs, Colette.
Nor bloodied trust of childhood,
spilled pathetically on hands we washed of you.
Infanticide became a pontius pact.

The die is cast, Colette, the mind is set.
We rally for your justice individually,
but pay your species scant regard.

Audrey Molloy

My Soul's Performance

Inside me is a vast theatre
with endless skies of stars above,
all around are tiers of steps,
dusty with age and lack of use,
one sole spectator - you.

And on the stage my heart and soul,
performing just for you.
I play, I dance, but mostly I sing,
and you clap your hands and stamp,
and throw flowers at my feet.

For you have your own ancient arena inside,
no need for instruments to breath or feed,
just a constant beat and a song,
so loud, surely everyone can hear?
Like a dying tree whose final bloom
is its most spectacular,
so is my soul's performance
for my special audience of one.
Who was last here?
When did they leave?

Audrey Molloy

The Fossil

The fossil forms slowly,
many years in the making,
the strata of sediment,
grain by small grain,
builds an unblemished imprint
of what lay before;
a mere crystallised cast
of the union remains.

A scaffold of papers,
of rings, dates and albums;
of copper and leather,
of willow and fruit;
replacing the tissues,
the bones and the organs,
subsuming the creature
in a mineral glue

that preserves every detail
of the union. Recording
every heartbeat and handhold,
each child's name they chose,
until after a decade
its form is immortal,
but the creature died softly,
eons ago.

Annette Mullumby

Seaweed

It seems like a piece of seaweed
caught in the sun net on the sand;
it rises through the pale green waves
into the loose bowl of my cupped hands.

Through the leafy stems of skin
I see the body of a yellow dragon
the current of its translucent fins
brushes my fingers.

As it sinks I'm drawn into
the sway and lilt of water;
whispers of the first sea
in the shell of my body.

Annette Mullumby

Teeth

Why don't you have teeth there
Nanna he says pointing to the gaps.

Oh I say they got worn out
chewing all those apples and nuts;

bored with being stuck in one spot
they hungered to explore new caves.

I tried to pep them up
twice a day they sang
to the twang of floss
squeaked when brushed clean;

but it wasn't enough
one by one they left.

Bring them back Nanna he sobs
bring them back.

At a loss I make two fingers teeth;
march them home.
They climb the cliff of my chin
roll on the tongue
sink into the their plush sockets
chatter to each other;

on my grandson's wet face, a wide smile.

Annette Mullumby

Trailing Clouds Of Glory*
for my grandson Gwydion

Spun from the ache of space;
a throb of light caught in carnal flesh
brushed by silken cilia,
you fall into the fertile valley.

From that first embrace
of cells, worlds uncurl
until limbs flower hands
to shape earth.

Muscles squeeze your head
against the bone barrier;
inch by inch you're pushed through.

to stark light on silk skin
your sharp cry shock of air
in startled lungs.

Now translucent sylph
you sleep swaddled
in our rough blankets.

* from *Ode: Intimations of Immortality* William Wordsworth

Karen Murphy

6 Months After My Friend Hangs Himself

Did they have to
untie the knot
you made?

The gap so tight,
so taut,
it felt more like they were
threading a needle,
trying not to get pricked
by the sharp touch of
death on the end.

Did they have to cut you
down?

The rope fraying,
split fibres
like an optical cord.

We saw you in high resolution,
cut through the connection,
rope blooming above them.

A black screen would have been
for mourning
but you never switched
the power off,
you just
decommissioned the show.

Now it's their job to
unplug you;
unwind you
from the coat rack
like a spool of cotton,

I was there
when they stitched you back
into the earth,
watched the thread disappear
around all the other
embroidered graves
and floral patterns.

Jan Napier

Other People's Love Poems

Women chime and stroke peacocks
men thunder and spur warhorses
in other people's love poems
lips lush as papayas ripen under Brazilian sun
breath scented with vanilla or liquorice
kisses like lightning strike sea water.
Lovers sprawl before logs of apple wood
muse misty woods   swim blue summers.
Sheets reek of musk and oyster
nights seethe in claret   ginger   lemon.

In my love poem there is a man.
He brings home grown apricots and grapes
grins and tips a snappy hat
paints me in sunflower and cirrus.
I offer green tea   ask his patience.

There is a man who looks at me sometimes
across a room   a page   a marriage.

K. K. O'Hara

Old Lace

Feelings by tender weave
Tendrils woven in the   ring
Promised   heart wings   bestowed
    The yellowed cloth
    With embroidered hem
    Precious when   he behove
        Her mirror-twirl   down
        Her mind's aisle   old
        Lace and pearl
            Frayed   holey   moth-whirls
            Nibbled knuckles   still nerves
            Enough to hold needles   and
                Feel the dimples
                Under his beard   and
                Black cow-licked hair
                      On the knit she wore   demure
                      Till he spun her arms   loose
                      And dyed her
                          Crochet sleeves
                          In cologne scent   blent
                          With camphor from the chest   and menthol
                              In the linen layers   preserved
                          A truer time
                          Without sepia proof

Kirsty Oehlers

You Started As An Ember

We are close enough to touch
but my hands feel as cool
as a thin sheet,
tremulous as a hatchling's wing.
I can't face you
in case my heart should slide
right on out.
I cup myself gently
like I'm holding sand.
There is so much of me
that flows outward.
Love is caught
on the jagged spires
of my lips
and the burning in my chest
starts scrubfires
in my throat.
I dampen myself
in the absence of you.

Jaya Penelope

You Knocked Out My Walls

put in windows that later
you would climb out of.
Here was the doorway
you will no longer walk
through. This is the space
I must build upon

the overturned
chair, a cup still warm
from your lips.

The roof I thatched with feathers
pulled from my own wings-
no two the same colour
the ladder I built of bone
laying fibula against femur.

You will never see
this, the way I put myself
back together, standing
on the foundations of this house
empty   singing.

Rachael Petridis

Come Closer
after Walt Whitman

let me feel the touch of your palm
soft pads of salve cool consoling—
smell the perfume of your breath
husked from youth
alive with syllables
spilling on the tongue

let me listen
to the wire of your chest
life-pulse to my leaning ear
fire in my ageing vein—

come closer to me
trace the forever story
seer   clairvoyant   palm
fingers   hand and arm
over and over

I want to shout stop
the hour   the day   the galloping year

Renee Pettitt-Schipp

Love Song

I cannot say what it is

but I have been circling it lately like a bird honing in on home, and my wings sing with its sight, with its colour, with the steady song that pulses through sky

Round and round I circle on its updraught, I am learning its rhythms and its sounds. Moving muscles slowly I find the wind new and clean on my face so I stay with the knowing of this song

Love and I, we are getting to know each other properly, but every day I see what each day I did not. Moving ever so slightly through her song-scape, I start to think of twigs and branches, but I do not think that love is a place where you can rest

So I work to be with love and I listen and I listen, soaring through her song, trying to be ready, to pay attention. And she is patient with me, we move together and I know one day

she will have me whole.

Margaret Owen Ruckert

In Love With An Ideal

She attends a prose writers' afternoon, more from curiosity than craft. Managed a few poems in print, longing for a style to emerge and become her, when a man walks up, completely unheralded.

Changes her forever. He was everything she'd missed in a man, physically strong, with humility in his talk, humour, and a smile that fired her inside. It was as if they'd slipped inside each other's pockets. Pockets that had known each other all their lives.

After the speeches and into red wine, he shares his memoir-cum-fiction experience with her. Would she like to see his first hundred pages? *Take them home. See what you think. I'd value the opinion of a poet. I also write poems.* He whips out his hand-written manuscript.

At home, she hunkers down with one more red and reads how a girl danced into his life, *completely unheralded* as he writes, and changed him forever. Thirty years ago. Thirty years ago, if only she'd been *the* girl, if only she'd been born overseas, exotic accent, wealthy parents, loving animals instead of knitting, been a stunner.

Why do men fall in love with stereotype, she asks, reading the explicit sections, again and again, the slender legs slipping through approving hands, his fingers never far from her long blond silk. His teenage romance, lost and rekindled, mid-fifties. This love affair, a one-sided story, like a plaything of a text. Little insight for a woman's needs.

She wants to ask the 'heroine', *how could you make love to this man, who's clearly just using you. You're his woman of the moment, he'll move on again. Love and loss repeat themselves with these men. He's not for bedding and wedding down. He's too bloody gorgeous.*

The poet sees potential in the writer's theme, but her frustration increases scene by scene. *Does this man know his reader audience? Fiction plays by rules, however carefree. Memoir has no contract with the truth. The only test – is it believable? Are the characters real or really remote?*

No meta-awareness she tells the cat. *When he sees the youth of his ways, his love could easily be brunette, filled-out, with character, a match for his quirks.* Her inner poet enjoys his lyric. But the dialogue he gives to his heroine is cold as a rival's tongue. It needs brutal help from one who knows – but she's brunette.

Francesca Sasnaitis

Ghazal For An American

A plaid shirt. A mild conversation. A sunstruck piazza.
                                      This is not love.
Assisi. Rocca Maggiore. The breath of summer on the wane.
                                      This is not love.

London Fields on the bench between us. He wants me
to tell him the story   *You're kidding, right?*
                                      This is not love.

Inhale. Exhale. Gather wits. Look into the distance.
Dredge up a performance for this American stranger
                                      This is not love.

And watch his face slide from polite interest to something
like surprise   *You're very articulate,* he says.
                                      This is not love.

I can almost hear him think   *she's not an airhead*
after all   I can almost hear him whisper that touch closer.
                                      This can't be love.

His move: he sings a song I've never heard before
of computational models of cognition and binary existence.
                                      This can't be love.

Santa Maria bless him. Bless me. Help me show him the grace
in San Francesco's outstretched hand   *Here, take mine.*
                                      This must be love.

Tim Sladden

The Holding Pattern

There *are* no coincidences in this apparent smattering of butterflies.
No notion of chance: Utter lies.
So, on cause and effect, pause   to reflect on *exactly* what this means.

(Perhaps)   You are not reading this by chance.   (Perhaps)
                 You were always going to read it.
                 Self. fulfilling. prophetic. genetics.

Yes, I have come to understand time
and I have come to understand time
defies understanding.

Like the greyhound chases the rabbit incessantly
                                    round and round in the dirt.
Time goes. And so I follow,
In order to understand.

I have waited. I have been in a holding pattern for you.
You, my element of consequence, precious Magnesium.
You see, as part of this empyrean dance
a circumstance has arisen whereby
you and I…   *wait!*
Did you do that to the sky?
It burns with the fire of a self-diagnosed apocalypse!
If it meant I could know time, I would follow you into that sun.

…You know, I do loathe the monogamy of space-time somewhat…

Why *can't* we move backwards - *no!*
                        s i d e w a y s through time?
To where in the world is Carmen Sandiego?!
To bodies with better circulation.
To a universe where I am a goat and you are a cat but we love each other anyway.
To a land made up entirely of hot springs, rain forests and Japanese restaurants.
We would heal ourselves there. In it, our programming waiting to be re-written.

Waiting. In a holding pattern. Circling high
                        Above the Callabonna salt flats.

Flora Smith

For My Brother

I was too young to help you then
too young   still crawling out of the box
of my upbringing   into a world where I was stiff-legged
scared as a young giraffe that knows
there are lions near.

When you left us
for those people with their games
and playthings we knew nothing of,
I was too self-absorbed to call you back
blinded by that inward eye of early marriage.
You left   determined to find danger in the world
to wring from it all the punishment you could.
You did it hard   hammering out a self
away from their ivied softness
from their blinkered view.

I was the dutiful daughter
builder of houses   mother of their grand-child.
I did it all   scaled those peaks of soft and narrow
touched up the mask   found it not so hard
to be oneself and love them too.   I sat for hours
in waiting rooms   worked through heavy documents
watched the backward staircase of old age
sitting with them every day towards the end.
I forged a life with them   loved them
and forgave them.

You never came:
the rationed phone call twice a year
                        all you had to give.

Yet some remaindered part
of love and time is surely ours now?
I need to storm your battlements   make a bonfire
of my anger   see all the sad swordplay
of our words and deeds
go up in flames.

I need to hear us speak with love
and talk forgiveness.

Elizabeth Tyson-Doneley

The Absence of Holding

I stood out on the footpath,
Streetlamps glowing,
The bare trees spidery with cold.
As the car you drove appeared
I felt scared, like hiding
In case it wasn't you.
The gravel glittered
In the spill of headlights,
The car still wet with dew.
In the cold winter morning
We drove away carefully,
Your face close to mine,
Arms covered in soft sleeves
Strong hands on the wheel.

The wing at my window,
Glistening white, the world below
A fairground of tiny lights,
And the heat of your body
Beside me, soft and reassuring,
Warm as the heart of a bird
In the icy cold of altitude,
My belly undone,
Hands loose in my lap.

Sitting now on the bus,
My fingers bare and aging,
I want suddenly to go home,
To nourish myself with comfort,
And keep my hands warm;
Safe in the absence of holding.

Tineke Van der Eecken

For Bert

I woke up this morning with an ant
tracing the sides of my palm
crossed and turned again

I woke up this morning thinking
of drawing circles in life
of twirling getting lost   how you and I
do that so well
each lost
in our own curve

I woke up this morning
soon not to be thinking   of you
About to crush the ant
I paused   placed my hand on the floor
let the ant go

Tineke Van der Eecken

In Winter

The colour red   like liver
bull's blood
in curled leaves

A river edged   by sediments,
withholding the yellows and greens of flowers,
the blues of berries
hiding the symbols of summer

Leaves have dropped
and cover the path
from your door to mine

I have forgotten about falling in love
like winter not knowing   who summer is

Winter sets in
I hold you in its frozen crust
waiting

Lyn Vellins

Dark Chocolates And Cherries

Give me wild nights of chocolates and cherries
let your kisses be red with the flesh of them
let them taste of dark nights in the forest.

Leave indelible marks on my body
slide along my secret trails leaving the taste
of tongue on fingertips navel hair toes.

Bathe in rose petals the colour of dark
cherries don't stop;
swallow the pits and I will swallow with you.

James Walton

Not Another Small Fucking Love Poem

This is how love ends:
I couldn't get anything right
So I gave up trying at all.
Stuck like a dingy out past
The breakers waiting to come in.
Watching you shoeless on the beach,
Annoyed at the sand I've become
Between your toes irritating
When it used to be a tickling joy.
My voice is a curlew now
Unmoving in the fog,
Persistent though, like Archimedes' principle
Held up in my hand hoping
For one more pass of the sand bar.

Julie Watts

This Is The Time I Like Best

with the heat receding
hot noon   giving way

dull sun   on the flapping blind
and black swans   flying   in our dreams.

The cliff of your body
hugging   my coastline

our loins   like small birds
nestled together   sleeping

your pale limbs   looping
and taking root.

This is the time –
our bodies on a crumpled landscape

breathing like rocks
facing   the same direction.

Sunny Wignall

De Grey River

Upriver trickles merge, engulfing
leaf and twig in silt
like blood, those lively things
are pulled in moon's unsteady lilt.

Each lunar whisper, steeped in spell
ensnares the mass in tune,
corralling will through seep and swell
to leap the ditch and dune.

But when the river's widening course
collects each bank with gush and,
lurching, snaps the girder's span,
then branch from source, the landscape falls.
And lovers, perching– stranded in their task:
"What cause, this swollen earth?", they ask.

Gail Willems

Fingertips

I
My fingertips step the spaces of your spine
remember each key   slowly measure the ache of you,
the space your name leaves.

II
The fragility of your commas
question marks   utterances   stray thoughts   photos;
I look for you with these fingers splayed on the page of a book
where once your voice traced a lattice of connections.

III
Step by step, toe to fingertip your memory slips
through eyes floated in tears   dissolving your tomorrows
will you stay long enough to know my touch tattoos love
across your skin

your fingers tap a rhythm   fumble on a breath
I'll leave the lights on for you to find me

Jena Woodhouse

Polydeuces

Who now recalls the colour of his eyes,
whether they matched the cobalt tesserae
scattered from rich mosaics of the villa's floor?
Perhaps they were blue, perhaps his hair
was fair, but all the extant likenesses
are monochrome. For Herod Atticus he was
the world — compared to such a love,
the world seemed colourless and small.

Mags Webster

My First Kiss

Was it Bill? Faded jeans, an experienced tongue—
or Tim—too tall, too shy—(but *nice*).
Or Jo? Same height, same age, same sex—
or Grace—fresh toothpaste, slow, polite.
Or was it John, the vicar's son—alleluia!—
(on my knees), or Chip, with stubble
on a rockstar chin? Was it deep and 'French'—
did my jaw go numb? Or was it furtive, rushed—
and somehow *wrong*? I remember the sound
of a saxophone, I remember the feeling
of flesh leaving bone. When I opened
up my eyes, too much light rushed in, so
I opened up my self, made the hurting begin.

Mags Webster

Strange Vernacular

That summer moon reminds me
we are in the season of haiku
when blossom snows the ground around the pool
and singing holds the colour of the air
I try to imagine myself as a lotus: sexual and mysterious
and I spend centuries perfecting my smile

at length, I realise this too may be futile
you have invented all the language we will ever need.

I've found when something's worth learning
I always resist it at first
you've taught me words which left their bite marks on my skin
carved your inventories on my spine
you've scoped me like landscape and I await
the brushstrokes of your breath, the weather of tongues

I'm still learning how to read your poetry,
how to ride into the blush of sunset.
At night you are an untamed garden
where I am abandoned to the trees.
They speak a strange vernacular,
each word an almond plashing to the ground
which splits and blooms into tiny cracks:
a new genealogy of speech

I worship you for your flavours
the umami of your flowers.

Beside you I am like a moth
which brims the shadows with flicker,
blots candlelight with its wings.
Calm as moon, you cup me in your hands
taste me syllable by syllable
phrase me tender as lychee.

This time, let me script you into my flesh,
wear you like small, perfect petals on my skin.

First published in *The Weather of Tongues* (Sunline Press, 2011)

Annamaria Weldon

Untrue Distinctions

> *I, you, he, she, we—*
> *in the garden of mystic lovers,*
> *these are not true distinctions.* Rumi

Because you are not a poet
and will never read this.
> *Though I have watched your hands, see that*
> *your fingers are shaped to make music or pictures.*

Because when you come to my house
I do not untie my hair.
> *You might want to lift its lengths from my shoulders,*
> *spread them like hanks of cloth, feel them*
> *slip silkwater from your cupped palms.*

Because I am not afraid to ask you
about the health of your fragile daughter.
> *Joy is unspoken between us,*
> *but let me share your sorrows.*

Because when I recall details from stories
you told me decades ago, it startles you.
> *Does a flower know that the bee*
> *makes honeycomb from its nectar?*

Because I always remember your birthday
and each year you have forgotten mine.
> *I walk barefoot through your thoughts*
> *and offer gratitude to your mother.*

Because you have held the worn hands of my parents
and felt my children's tender wrists
but never invited us to your home.
> *If you are expected, I rub sandalwood*
> *into my hair, oil of angelica on my throat*
> *and wrists, fill the rooms with fragrant incense.*

Because when we met, so long ago
that both of us still had black hair, only
you asked me if I had been to India.
> *Can a question predict the past, outguess*
> *the future, just as a bird at take-off*
> *prefigures all manner of flight?*

Annamaria Weldon

Because when I offer coffee, and you accept
the cup, I sit on the far sofa to drink mine.
There is no separation, only the illusion of separateness.

Sean M. Whelan

They Don't Love Blue

Tell me where to stand in the garden.
And I'll mark the spot.
You'll find me there every evening at dusk.
Watching the day transmogrify, just like we did.

Tell me where the light falls the best upon my face.
I want to be just as handsome as you are supernatural.
Just because I don't believe in permanence
doesn't mean I want to forget this.
I want to build a theme park to us in the mountains of my mind,
travel there every lonely hour and take all the rides.
Tell me where to stand in the garden.
Where nobody will see us.
Not even Lou Reed's satellites.
Tell me this shit is real.
Or unreal.
That works too.

Show me a species of bird that migrates from Melbourne to Manhattan every year
and I'll tie a love letter around its ankle.
Tell me, do birds even have ankles?
Tell me how somebody so old could still be learning about birds.
And by that I mean actual birds, but the other way works too.
Tell me how you know so much stuff.
I want this love to have its own Wikipedia entry.
I want the New York Times to tell me we're getting married.
I want to be more famous than your dresses.
I only want to live long enough to know how to die right.

Let's synchronise our watches so we break up at the same time.
Then let's drown our watches in the kitchen sink, so that we never break up.
I know, we broke up, but for the purpose of this poem, let's pretend that we didn't.
Or let's write up a post-breakup agreement with plenty of day passes.
Then let's swap shadows, so I can watch your determined walk all the time.

Tell me where to stand in the garden.
Light has the highest concentration of magic at dusk.
Fact.
We can dig in here forever.
We can learn how to grow.
Tell me where the soil is the softest, where the underworld will receive us the quickest.
I have the best of friends in low places.

Sean M. Whelan

I'm sorry the love letter I wrote you was eaten by the sky.
How could I know the future could eat so much?

Tarkovsky wrote poems with a camera.
He knew about us
That we would break up.
He knew we didn't need to worry about this.
And he was right.
When those doe-eyed, beared boy scouts come at you
With a pocket full of sadsong mixtapes.
Wait and remember
they don't love blue like I do.

Sean M. Whelan

This Is How It Works

Where were you baby, when the calendar became the carpet beneath my feet?
I looked at my watch, with five seconds to nowhere on New Years Eve, my watch looked back
but it couldn't speak.
Turned my mind instead to that day you stook half naked in a field of wheat.

We only stopped the car to look at a tree.
Shaped like a dry brown witches claw.
Reaching up towards the clouds, trying to steal the future
from god's underwear draw.

Some say that's when the year really ended.
And by some, I mean nobody at all.
Some scientists say the sun is shrinking all the time.
And by some, I do mean some.
I dreamt our time together was long enough to watch it snuff out like a candle.
Hand in hand witnesses to the ultimate celestial scandal.
But it wasn't.

Most of my favourite writers love to speak of hunting and fishing.
I have never done either and most likely never will.
Unless vegetables were to gain self-awareness.
And the ability to flee from cutlery.
But the fact is, we're all capable of everything.

Lost my art in San Francisco.
Wrestled with feral cats.
While you were going to a go-go.
But it's really no matter.

The lackaday.
Is already fading away.
Sliding down the heartbreak scale
From black to grey.

This, is how it works.
This is how time begins, starts and stops.
This is what gives time a bad back.
This is what black holes are for.
Where else is all that wretched sorrow going to go?
These are the lays of our lives.
And there's no reason that holds any grain of genuine deep soul truth
to be unhappy about that.

Sean M. Whelan

Let's do it all over again.
Last one to leave, turns out the sun.

Tom Lanoye

Analyse

Het zijn slechte tijden voor de
poëzie. De mensen zijn gelukkig.
Zij leven niet voor woorden, en
geef ze daarin maar eens ongelijk.
Waarom zou iemand vandaag de dag
nog lezen? Statistisch is bewezen
dat waar armoe en verdrukking zijn
verdwenen, het met de kwaliteit
van de gedichten niet veel beter is
gesteld. Er valt niets te vertolken in
het voetlicht van tevreden volken.

Nu zult u zeggen: godzijdank
is er altijd nog de zekerheid
dat ook zonder oorlog iedereen
de pijp uitgaat. En dat men, zo
die wens bestaat, intussen zelfs
kan lijden aan wat klein gemier.
Zoals aan het onhandige kanaliseren
van de driften die wij liefde
noemen. Maar zonder dat schreef
niemand hier één vers de moeite
van het schrijven waard. Ook

ik, die dichter ben in deze poel
van gezelligheid en rust. Ben
ik wel een dichter? Is
wat ik schrijf oprecht
datgene wat ik schrijf? Of
spreekt het enkel het verlangen
van zijn maker uit, te zijn
wat ik niet ben: symbool
van grootse tijden, een
sterveling die blijft,
een engel met een pen?

First published in *DE MEESTE GEDICHTEN* (Prometheus, Amsterdam, 2005)

Tom Lanoye

Analysis

These are bad times for
poetry. People are happy.
They don't live for words, and
who should blame them for it?
Why would anyone these days
read? Statistics have shown
that where poverty and oppression
have disappeared, the quality of poetry
is not doing much better.
There is not much to be voiced
on the boards of satisfied people.

Now you will say: thank God
for the absolute certainty
that even without war, everyone
will kick the bucket. And meanwhile,
should the wish exist, one
can suffer from minor muddling.
Like the clumsy channeling
of the urges we call
love. But without this no one here
would pen down even one verse
worth writing. Not even

me, who is a poet in this cesspool
of cosiness and quiet. Am I
really a poet? Is
what I write genuinely
what I write? Or
does it only speak of the desire
of its creator, to be
what I am not: a symbol of
glorious times, a
mortal lives on,
an angel with a pen?

Translation: Katia Brys and Tineke Van der Eecken

Tom Lanoye

Beknopte Evolutieleer

Bedreig mij nooit met eenzaamheid. Zonder jou
kan ik nog altijd oude dames naaien en daarna
vriendschap sluiten met hun hond. Er zijn ook één
miljard Chinezen en vliegen nog veel meer, dus mij
chanteer je niet met isoleren. Als *ik* capituleer,

dan is het voor te veel. Voor één miljard Chinezen,
en vliegen steeds maar meer. Al die onbeschreven
levens in een kluwen, een aquarium vol gier
dat als een draaikolk aan mij trekt en mij
zonder naam verteert. Daarvoor ben ik bang.

En dit. Als je me verlaat, verdrink ook jij, met
geen pen weer op te vissen uit diezelfde brij. Dus
blijf. Het is een kwestie van survival, ook voor mij.
Want als ik jou niet langer kan beschrijven, schiet
ik mij liever door de kop. Ik hang mij op — why

not? Een leven min, een
leven meer. Er zijn één
miljard Chinezen. En al
die vliegen dan, mijnheer.

First published in *DE MEESTE GEDICHTEN* (Prometheus, Amsterdam, 2005)

Tom Lanoye

Concise Theory Of Evolution

Never threaten me with solitude. Without you
I can still screw old ladies and after that
make friends with their doggies. There are also one
billion Chinese, and flies a lot, lot more, so you can't
blackmail me with isolation. If *I* ever capitulate,

it's because of too many. *Because of* one billion Chinese,
and flies still more and more. All these undescribed
lives in a jumble, an aquarium full of liquid manure
that pulls at me like a whirlpool and namelessly
consumes me. That's what scares me.

And this. Leaving me will also drown you, with
no pen to fish you up from that brew. So
stay. It's a matter of survival for me, too.
'Cause if I can't describe you any longer,
I'll blow my head off. I'll hang myself, why

not? One life less, one
life more. There are one
billion Chinese. And flies,
Sir, flies galore.

Translation: Bart Eeckhout and Tom Lanoye

Tom Lanoye

Zindelijkheidstraining

Net voor ik voorgoed uit Gent vertrek, een laatste
glas gaan drinken in Café Cirque Central, en hé!
Het snookerbiljart is gerepareerd! En, als door
het Lot georkestreerd, bemand, dat is het woord.
Met twee jonge gasten, jeunesse dorée, de een
al geiler dan de ander, elk om beurt over het laken
buigend met gespannen billen, stoot na stoot. En daar

is ze weer, even plots en onontkoombaar als
misselijkheid op zee, die eeuwige rotidee.
Dat wij, totterdood, een samenspel van zweet
en speeksel, zaad en slijmen, passie heten,
en dat het ons tot wanhoop drijft. Ik heb daar
al veel over nagedacht, vooral op café, maar
begrijpen? Nee. Ik zal er dan maar weer 's over

schrijven, allez vooruit: Lik mijn stijve lik
mijn kont geef de asbak eens door schat
je bent geweldig mwaaw hwaal he hwoet
uid mwijn mwond met je lekkere met je
lekkere dinges enfin hoe heet het ook
alweer auw pas op je doet me pijn...

Fantastisch toch, dat
er gedichten zijn.

First published in *DE MEESTE GEDICHTEN* (Prometheus, Amsterdam, 2005)

Tom Lanoye

House-Training

Before leaving Ghent for good, I jumped into
Café Cirque Central, for a final one for the road,
and hey! The pool table had been repaired! And,
as if orchestrated by Fate, manned — that is the
word. By two young blokes, *gilded youth,* the one
even sexier than the other, each in turn leaning over
the cloth with tense buttocks, shot after shot. And

there it is again, as sudden and inescapable as
nausea at sea, that eternally shitty idea. That we,
till death do us part, declare an interplay of
sweat and spit, sperm and phlegm, our passion,
and that it drives us to despair. I've thought
about this often, mainly in cafés, but did I ever
understand it? No. So let me, once again, just

write about it, shoot: Lick my hard-on lick
my ass pass the ashtray will you honey
you're the best bwud gwed yoa fwoot
oud of mwy mwouf with your sweet with
your sweet little hell whatchamacallit ouch
watch out you bitch you're hurting me...

Fantastic are, won't you agree?, the pains
and powers of poetry.

Translation: Bart Eeckhout and Tom Lanoye

Tom Lanoye

Poker

Het is tijd voor open spel, mijn
liefste. De kaarten op de tafel. Ik heb
er twee: mijzelf en wat ik schrijf. Ze
zijn van weinig waarde, om niet
te zeggen van geen tel. De

hand van jou is rijker, je lijf
is nog het minste, al is het lang
niet mis. Maar ook illusies heb
jij nog, en hoop. Jij hebt alles
wat er is. Toch ben ik soms al

op je uitgekeken, ontkennen heeft
geen zin. Je zult dat ook wel weten:
gewenning is een ziekte, ze slaat
toe van bij het begin, en op het
einde is het beter om te breken.

Ik wil daar nu niet over praten.
Wat komen moet, dat komt. Alleen:
er zal nimmer sprake zijn van schuld.
En nog minder van vergeten. Dat er, in
dit land van kwezels en kastraten,

in deze tijd van tegenstand en
onbenul, twee levens waren die
elkander kruisten, met een vuurwerk
van vergeefse woorden, en de troost
van wat lichamelijk tumult.

First published in *DE MEESTE GEDICHTEN* (Prometheus, Amsterdam, 2005)

Tom Lanoye

Poker

It's time to play open game, my
love. Cards on the table. I have
two: myself and what I write. They
are of little value, not to
say of no account. That

hand of yours is richer, your body not
even your trump card, though it's not bad
at all. But you cherish illusions still,
and hope. You have everything
there is. Yet sometimes I get

tired of you, there's no point
denying it. You must know this well:
routine is an infection, it breaks
out from the start, and in the
end we'd rather break apart.

I don't want to discuss this now.
What will be will be. Just this:
Never will we talk of guilt. Less
even of forgetting. That, in this
realm of hypocrites and eunuchs,

in this climate of adversity and
ignorance, there once were two lives
that crossed one another, with fireworks
of futile words, and the comfort
of some physical upheaval.

Translation: Katia Brys and Tineke Van der Eecken

Tom Lanoye

Programma

Weet ik veel hoe poëzie eruit
moet zien. Niet dat statische,
dat uniforme. Daar hou ik niet
zo van. Dezelfde toon herhaald
tot in den treure, en dat dan
'vormvastheid' noemen, of 'een
eigen stem', dat soort gelul.
Nee, daar hou ik niet zo van.

Geef mij dan maar het favoriete
snoepgoed uit mijn jeugd. De
toverbal. Je zuigt en zuigt
maar, telkens komen er andere
kleuren te voorschijn en voor
je 't weet, heb je helemaal
niets meer. Dát is het, vind
ik. Zoiets. Ongeveer.

First published in *DE MEESTE GEDICHTEN* (Prometheus, Amsterdam, 2005)

Tom Lanoye

Programme

I have no idea what poetry should
look like. Not that static thing,
that uniformity that I
dislike. The endless repetition
of the same tone, and calling it
'compliance to form', or 'one's
own voice', that kind of crap.
No, I don't tend to enjoy that.

I'd rather have the favorite
candy of my youth. The
gobstopper. You suck and suck,
each time new colours
appear and before you
realize, there's nothing
left. That's it, I think.
Thereabout. More or less.

Translation: Katia Brys and Tineke Van der Eecken

Tom Lanoye

Rebellie

als actie geen optie is wat rest ons dan tenzij
het engelengezang van wanhopigen die zijn ontdaan
van een geslacht dat ze niet bezaten in the first place

neem tegen beter weten
geen vrede met de vrede
alles is nog altijd mogelijk

nog één keer wil ik barsten en vergaan
nog één keer de spijker zijn waaraan ik
me verscheur — en daarna nog een keer

toch weer de vlam zijn die het vuur kan
verzengen de vis die de zee verdrinkt
en omgekeerd — en daarna opnieuw

telkens weer
eens te meer

eindeloos beginnen
voor de eerste keer

heldhaftig en gehaast zoals het meisje
dat met haar eerste menstruatiebloed
haar eerste liefdesbrief begint aan
de man die ze nog niet heeft ontmoet

Tom Lanoye

Rebellion

when action is no option, then what is left
beside
the angelic singing of the desperate
stripped
of a gender they never had in the
first place

don't be at peace with peace
against your better judgement
everything is still possible

one more time I'd like to burst and perish
one more time be the nail that
tears me – and then once more

be again the flame that scorches
the fire the fish that drowns the sea
and vice versa – and then, again

time and again
yet again

endlessly beginning
for the first time

heroically and hastily like the girl
who with her first menstrual blood
writes her first love letter to
the man she has not yet met

Translation: Katia Brys and Tineke Van der Eecken

Tom Lanoye

Laaglied

Heer, wij bidden u. Maak door verdwazing
onze dagen korter. Dan zijn ze makk'lijker te
dragen. Ruk het bewustzijn uit ons hoofd
en hang het te drogen aan een vleeshaak
boven de toog.

Sla ons, trap ons in elkaar, o Grote Poten
rammer. Dat uw pijn onze hersens verdove
met de geur van onmacht en bloed. Laat ons
ruiken, heel even, aan de wil tot overleven
als aan een oksel.

Of verdrink ons, Heer. Ik noem maar wat. Dat
wij, door de zee verworpen vissen, eind'lijk
zouden vechten tegen de onmeet'lijkheid
van uw waters, door onze longen daartoe
gedwongen.

En als dat niet kan, stuurt u dan
maar iemand om ons af te zuigen. Ze mogen
met twee zijn ook. Alweer tien seconden om
aan niets te denken, aan niets dan aan
nog tien seconden

en ik kom. Hallellllujaaaaaaaaahhhhhhhhhh.
Stel, Heer, stél: dat onze geest orgasme werd,
en andersom. Leven onder de narcose van
permanent zaad te kunnen lozen, met slechts
af en toe,

als hoogtepunt van minnespel, het
wurgende besef van de banaliteit
van het bestaan. Zou dat niet gaan, o Heer?
Gij die alles kunt. Hebt u dat nergens
op uw blaadje staan?

First published in *DE MEESTE GEDICHTEN* (Prometheus, Amsterdam, 2005)

Tom Lanoye

Song Of Songs

Lord, we pray Thee. Through infatuation
shorten our days. So they'll be easier to
stand. Tear consciousness out of our heads
and hang it high to dry on a meat hook
above the counter.

Hit us, beat us up, O Great Queer-
Basher. That Thy pain may numb our brains
with the tang of impotence and blood. Let us
smell, for one split second, at the will
to survive as at an armpit.

Or drown us, Lord. Whatever. That we,
fish rejected by the sea, at last will
fight the immeasurability of Thy
waters, in despair of gasping
for air.

And if that not, then send us someone
for a blow job. There may be two of them
to boot. Oh! Another ten seconds to think
about nothing, about nothing but another
ten seconds

and I'm coming. Hallelllujaaaaaahhhh. Suppose,
Lord, *suppose:* that our mind became an orgasm,
and the other way around. To live under the
narcosis of permanently passing our semen,
with only now

and then, as the peak of this our courtly love, the
strangling sense of the banality of this our life.
Would that be too much of a strife, o Lord? Thou who
canst do everything. Canst Thou not carve it on a table
with Thy knife?

Translation: Bart Eeckhout and Tom Lanoye

Tom Lanoye

The Absence Of Hierarchies

Naarmate de uren versnellen
als propellers
en de dagen gaten slaan
als hamers,
wordt mijn angst bewoonbaar,

mijn keuze helder.
Laat de zee maar branden
als olie in een vat,
laat alle muren kantelen.
Er is maar één ding

dat ik wil bewaren:
de klaver van jouw keel,
de papaver van je lippen.

En van elke stoot dit beeld:
de honing van je oksel, de
melk uit je schoot, en

de schaduw van kaneel
die mij vangt als
ik jou streel.

First published in *DE MEESTE GEDICHTEN* (Prometheus, Amsterdam, 2005)

Tom Lanoye

The Absence Of Hierarchies

As the hours quicken
like propellers
and the days make dents
like hammers,
my fears become habitable,

my choices clear.
Let the sea burn
like petrol in a drum,
let all walls tumble
There's but one thing

that I would like to keep:
the clover of your throat,
the poppy of your lips.

And of each thrust this image:
the honey of your armpit, the
milk from your loins, and

the cinnamon shadow
that captures me
while I do caress you.

Translation: Katia Brys and Tineke Van der Eecken

Biographies

Carolyn Abbs has published poems most recently in *Westerly, Cordite, Sotto, Rabbit* and *The Best Australian Poems 2014*. Her poetry has won prizes; and she was awarded a FAWWA mentorship (2013). Her PhD is from Murdoch University where she taught in the School of Arts for a number of years.

Atheer Al-Khalfa is an engineer from Adelaide, but he reads and writes for a living. His work has been published online with *Australian Poetry* and *Ricochet Magazine* and in print in various anthologies such as the *Offset Journal* of Victoria University and *Visible Ink* of RMIT.

Australian born **Richard James Allen's** recent collection of poems, *Fixing the Broken Nightingale* (Flying Island Books) is his tenth book as a poet, fiction, performance writer and editor: http://www.fixingthebrokennightingale.com/. Widely published in anthologies, journals and online, Dr Allen is a multi-award-winning writer, director, choreographer, scholar and educator: www.physicaltv.com.au

Meg Caddy has a BA in English Literature and History from the University of Western Australia. In 2013, her YA fantasy novel *Waer* was shortlisted for the Text Prize, which led to a contract with Text Publishing. Meg was the 2013 Young Writer-in-Residence at the Katharine Susannah Prichard Writers' Centre.

Liana Joy Christensen has been widely published. In 2010, she won the Peter Cowan's Patron's Prize for Poetry. In 2011, she was Biodiversity Poet in Residence at the Flourish Festival. Her work appears in the *Performance Poets 3*, Fremantle Press 2013. She was editor of *Poetry d'Amour*, 2014 and shortlisted for the Newcastle Poetry Prize in 2014.

Julie Clark was born in North Fremantle in1958. First poem published 1987. Wrote satirical plays for radio in the 90's. First book published 2012, *WX289*. Being a war widow means she can now devote most of her time to writing.

Rose Crocker is currently a first year student undertaking a Bachelor of Science(Adv.) at The University of Adelaide. Although she is studying environmental science, poetry has always been a passion of hers. Rose hopes to combine her love of writing and the environment in her future pursuits.

Peter Curry is a lawyer who also writes, but as he matures he sees less and less difference between the various forms of wordsmithing. Peter also likes to walk, talk, drink young Pinot and older Cabernet, eat, cook, sing and talk some more, and love of course, but don't we all.

Cuttlewoman started writing poetry because she fell in love with a friend's father and did not know where to go with that! Using a pseudonym suits her because it gives her some distance between her everyday life and the person she thinks of as the poetess. A lot of the time poetry is where she puts things that hurt. Other times, writing poetry is just being silly.

Gary Colombo De Piazzi enjoys exploring the magic and power of words and holds executive positions on the committees of WA Poets Inc. and Creative Connections Art & Poetry Exhibitions.

Biographies

Audrey El-Osta is a Melbourne born writer and student. She studies a BA in Psycholinguistics at Monash University, is the Vice President of the Creative Writers Club, and has loved language passionately since childhood. She aims to publish a collection of confessional poetry, exploring sexuality, mental illness and comedy.

Frances Faith is the lucky child of a father who read her Eloise and Dr Seuss, and a mother with a passion for dance and theatre. She enjoys many forms of writing, including drama scripts, short stories, non-fiction and poetry. She is a home-educating mother of nine and is currently conducting her magnificent life on the south-western shores of Terra Australis.

Michelle Faye currently resides in Mt Lawley, Western Australia and has recently completed a Bachelor of Arts in Creative Writing at Murdoch University. Her short story *Blowie* was published in *Regime 02* and her short story *Father* received a commendation for the KSP Short Fiction Awards and can be found in *Tincture Journal's Issue Two*. As well as writing fiction she turns her hand to poetry. Some of her words can be found amongst the pages of *Poetry d'Amour 2013*, released by WA Poets Inc.

Kevin Gillam is a West Australian born writer with three books of poetry published, *other gravities* (2003) and *permitted to fall* (2007) both with Sunline Press, and *songs sul G* in *Two Poets* (2011) with Fremantle Press. He has also had three chapbooks published by Picaro Press; *shouting, drowning; closer to now* and *The Seasons*. He works as Director of Music at Christ Church Grammar School.

Fran Graham's passions are poetry, reading and learning. She has been published in journals and anthologies including *Westerly, Poetry d'Amour* and *Best Australian Poems 2012*. Her first collection, *On a Hook Behind the Door*, was published by Ginninderra Press in 2011. She is currently studying for her Masters in Applied Linguistics.

Danny Gunzburg has been writing songs and poems since his early teens. In 1995 he was appointed Emerging Writer-In-Residence at The Katharine Susannah Pritchard Writers Centre. Since then, he has been entertaining audiences at Perth Poetry Club and other venues in Perth with his poetry and music. In 2014 he won "commended" awards in both the Poetry d'Amour Contest and The WAPI Song Lyric Contest.

Helen Hagemann has two collections of poetry, *Evangelyne & Other Poems* (APC, 2009) and of *Arc & Shadow* (Sunline Press, 2013).

Lorraine Haig is a textile artist and poet. She has a fine arts degree from the University of Tasmania and lives with her husband in the historic village of Richmond. Her work has been published in poetry magazines and anthologies as well as online. Her first poetry book will be released soon.

Ron Heard enjoys life in Brisbane among the heat, rain and backyard chooks. He cares for an adult disabled son and edits *The Mozzie,* an independent poetry magazine that publishes over 400 poems a year. His most recent publication is a verse novel *The Shadow of Troy.*

Biographies

Ross Jackson lives a small life in Churchlands but enjoys attending OOTA classes and is a regular at Voicebox. He writes a lot of poetry about isolated figures in suburban landscapes. Awarded second prize in Poetry d'Amour 2014, his poems have appeared on websites and in literary journals.

Kerryn M. Kapitola is a Perth-based writer, barista and mystery shopper. She travels the world, collecting Wi-Fi codes and splits her free time between making her friends laugh and discussing what it means to be a woman, sometimes in Spanish.

Christopher Konrad is a Western Australian writer and has poems and short stories published in many journals and on line. He has received many awards for his writing and his recent book *Letters to Mark* was published by Regime Books, 2014. He currently teaches Social Sciences in Melbourne

Deeksha Koul currently lives in Perth and is from Kashmir, India. Curious to explore what she can say with the English language, she has been writing free verse poetry since 2013. In 2014, she completed her undergraduate degrees in Civil Engineering and Law from the University of Western Australia.

Veronica Lake is a Literature teacher. She collates and edits the student poetry journal *Primo Lux,* now in its eleventh year. In 2010 she was awarded a Churchill Fellow, to study Shakespeare. She believes creativity is the best method of teaching, as it promotes understanding and enjoyment of language.

Tom Lanoye was born in Sint-Niklaas, Northern Belgium in 1958. Lanoye, who is highly regarded for both his poetry and theatre work, started his career as a performer in cafés and as the publisher of his own poems. He has since become one of the most well-known Flemish writers. Lanoye's novels, poems, and shows are typified by his strong rhetorical ability and his sharp sense of humour.

Wes Lee lives in New Zealand. Her debut collection *Cowboy Genes* was published by Grist Books at the University of Huddersfield in 2014. She was the 2010 recipient of The BNZ Katherine Mansfield Literary Award. Her poetry has recently appeared in *Poetry London, Magma, Riptide, Westerly, Landfall,* and *Dazzled: The University of Canberra Vice-Chancellor's Poetry Prize Anthology.* More information can be found at her website: www.weslee.co.nz

louisa draws inspiration from ordinary people and life events in ordinary lives. Inspiration from her earthy environment combined with memory and imagination creatively mixed then distilled, are features of her work.

Shey Marque holds a Master of Arts in creative writing from Swinburne University in Melbourne and has published poetry in literary journals and anthologies including *Australian Love Poems 2013, Award Winning Australian Writing 2014, Westerly* and *Regime*. In 2013 she won the Karen W Treanor Poetry Prize.

Shane McCauley has had seven books of poetry published, including *The Drunken Elk* (Sunline Press, 2010) with an eighth forthcoming, *Trickster* (Walleah Press). He has won the Tom Collins and Max Harris poetry prizes, and

Biographies

won first prize in the 2014 Poetry d'Amour competition. In 2014 he celebrates 10 happy years as a poetry tutor with the OOTA Writers' Group.

Fiona McIlroy has published a collection *Taste of a Poem* (Ginninderra Press 2009) with poems in several anthologies, including *Poetry d'Amour* and *Australian Love Poems 2014*. She won first prize HRAFF Poetry competition 2009, and convenes Poetry in Motion biennial Poets Train. As coach, mediator, grandparent, she celebrates relationship.

Max Merckenschlager is a retired teacher, including 2 years in Yemen Arab Republic, agriculturalist and native seed harvester. His two books *Lifemarks* and *Captured Moments* (Ginninderra Press) contain 4 Grenfell statuette winners, a Rolfe Boldrewood award and 3 national ABPA championship-winning poems.

Audrey Molloy On a recent trip to her native Ireland, Audrey discovered a book of poems she wrote when she was eight years old. 33 years later, poetry returned when she woke one morning with a poem fully formed in her head, and they just keep coming. Audrey lives in Sydney with her young family.

Annette Mullumby was born in London during World War II. Graduated from U.W.A. with a degree in poetry and for many years taught upper school English Literature then reskilled as a psychotherapist. Trained in Japanese Butoh, she loves creating dance in response to landscape, particularly the beach. Now retired, she devotes her time to her first love poetry and is writing a memoir.

Karen Murphy is the Pen name for Karen Lowry, a PhD student at Curtin University working in poetry and electronic literature. She blogs at www.karenlouisemurphy.com

Jan Napier lives near the Indian Ocean. Her poetry has been showcased in *Poetry d'Amour, Westerly, The Stars Like Sand, Windfall 2, Regime* and *Unusual Work*, plus other journals and anthologies both here and overseas.

Kirsty Oehlers is a new writer of creative works and she also works as a social worker, writing about the real lives of people. She blends her love of the unseen world, with the world before our eyes. Her poetry was published last year for the first time in *White Ash Literary Magazine*.

K. K. O'Hara is a poet and public servant based in Canberra. She has recently returned from three years living in Japan.

Rachael Petridis is a Western Australian poet. She has published nationally in literary journals and anthologies. In 2009 she won a place at Varuna Longlines Australian Poetry Workshop, NSW. Her first collection *Sundecked* (Australian Poetry Centre) received a commendation in the Anne Elder award. Recent commended poems include *Breathing Flower,* Spilt Ink Poetry Prize 2012 and *Child's Play,* Tom Collins Prize 2013.

Jaya Penelope; poet and storyteller, Jaya's work is nourished by her endless fascination with folklore, fairytale and mythology. A published poet, her first love remains the spoken word. She is also a lover of walking, wild figs and

Biographies

sunset storms. She can sometimes be seen telling stories with her band of bards *the Tealeaf Troubadours*...

Renee Pettitt-Schipp has lived in the Indian Ocean Territories for the past three years, however 2014 saw her return to the port city of Fremantle she calls home. Over the past four years Renee has been shortlisted for the ACU Poetry Prize as well as the Trudy Graham Biennial Literary Award, and has won and been shortlisted in the Ethel Webb Bundell Prize for Poetry. Renee is currently enjoying bringing her work into the public sphere through performance and artistic collaborations.

Margaret Owen Ruckert, educator and poet, is widely published. Her book *musefood* won the 2012 IP Poetry Book of the Year. Her first book *You Deserve Dessert* explored sweet foods. A previous winner of NSW Women Writers National Award, Margaret gives writing workshops as Facilitator of Hurstville Discovery Writers.

Anna Ryan-Punch is a Melbourne poet and critic. Her previously published poetry includes work in *Island, Quadrant, The Age, Overland, Southerly, Antipodes* and *Westerly*.

Francesca Sasnaitis is a Melbourne-based writer and artist, currently embarked on a PhD in Creative Writing at the University of Western Australia. Her poetry, fiction and reviews have most recently appeared in *Australian Book Review, Cordite, Southerly, Sydney Review of Books, The Trouble with Flying and other stories* and *Westerly*.

Tim Sladden, guitarist and songwriter, had until recently simply used music as a means for expression. Instinctively focusing on his lyrical content meant that poetry was never too far around the corner.

Flora Smith has been published in journals and anthologies around Australia, such as *Westerly, indigo* and *Sotto* and was selected for the Australian Poetry Cafe Poet program for 2013. She has won several prizes for her poetry and has had 2 volumes of poetry published. Flora's poems are stories about people - their failings, hopes and dreams.

Elizabeth Tyson-Doneley is a writer of plays, poetry and memoir living in Brisbane. She is also a production designer in film and has a tendency to bring strange objects home 'in case they could be used for something.' She is currently cleaning out her studio and reading piles of books.

Tineke Van der Eecken is a Belgian-born West Australian who writes poetry and creative non-fiction. She has lived in Africa and Europe before a turn in her personal life brought her to Western Australia. Her poetry is published in Australia, NZ and the UK. Tineke is one of the instigators for Poetry d'Amour.

Rose van Son's poems, stories and articles have appeared in many journals including *Cordite, Australian Poetry, Westerly, Indigo, JukeBox, Prospect Four* and more. She has won prizes in the Tom Collins Poetry Prize (2013), the W.H. Treanor Poetry Prize, the Peter Cowan Patron's Prize. Her haiku have appeared in *paper wasp, The Heron's Nest and One Hundred Gourds.* Her poetry collection

Biographies

appears in *Sandfire,* (2011), and another in *Three in the Campagna,* (2014). She is Haiku editor for *Creatrix* online, and is working on a new manuscript. Rose has judged several poetry prizes and gives presentations and writing workshops.

Lyn Vellins , is a Sydney-based published poet. She runs a monthly poetry reading group, 'RhiZomic' and was on the committee of many reputed publications and several editorial committees whilst at Sydney University. She is a current member of Australian Poetry's National Advisory Council. Her first collection of poetry, *A Fragile Transcendence*, was published by Picaro Press in July, 2012.

James Walton is from South Gippsland. His work has appeared in many publications and The Age Newspaper. He was shortlisted for The ACU National Literature Prize in 2013 and commended in The Welsh Poetry Competition 2014. He began writing poetry again in 2013, having been a public sector union official for 29 years.

Julie Watts is a WA writer and Play Therapist. She is a member of OOTA, a Fremantle based writer's group and has been published in various anthologies and journals including *Poetry d'Amour 2013, 2014*. Julie's first collection of poetry, *Honey & Hemlock*, was published in 2013 by Sunline Press.

Mags Webster's first collection of poetry, *The Weather of Tongues* (Sunline Press), won the 2011 Anne Elder Award. Her poetry and prose has been published in various publications and anthologies in Australia and Asia. Mags moved from the UK to Perth in 2003, and is currently based in Hong Kong

Annamaria Weldon is a West Australian poet and essayist. Her landscape memoir *The Lake's Apprentice* was published in 2014 by UWA Publishing. She has won several awards including the Tom Collins Poetry Prize and the inaugural Nature Conservancy Australia Essay Competition, and was shortlisted for the Peter Porter Poetry Prize.

Sunny Wignall began writing in his early 20's, having frequented Smash Mouth and New Word Order poetry clubs. He is currently pursuing post-graduate studies in creative writing at Curtin University. Apart from this, he enjoys writing songs for his band, Crying Town, and works in the counselling field.

Gail Willems is a retired nurse living in Mandurah and swims, writes poetry and loves good shiraz. She has been published in journals, magazines, on radio and anthologies (including academic), in N.Z. Belgium, Australia. Winner Poetry D'Amour 2013, Peel Region Winner 2014, First poetry collection *Blood Ties and Crack-Fed Dreams* published by Ginninderra Press November 2013

Jena Woodhouse was shortlisted in the Montreal International Poetry Prize 2013 and the ACU Prize for Literature 2013; longlisted in the University of Canberra Vice-Chancellor's International Poetry Prize 2014. Her translations from the Russian of poems by Vera Pavlova and Olga Sedakova appear on the Red Room site http://redroomcompany.org/projects/lyrikline-collaboration/ and also on Lyrikline.org (Berlin). She was a Hawthornden Fellow (2011) and on retreat at La Muse (France) in 2014.

Printed in Australia
AUOC02n1038281014
263963AU00006B/8/P